27158

TENZIN GYATSO
THE DALAI LAMA

WORLD LEADERS   PAST AND PRESENT

TENZIN GYATSO
THE DALAI LAMA

Kai Friese

HARRAP

London

First published in the United States of America 1989
© 1989 by Chelsea House Publishers
a division of Main Line Book Co.
Introduction © 1985 by Arthur M Schlesinger, jr.
This edition first published in Great Britain 1990
by Harrap Books Ltd
Chelsea House, 26 Market Square,
Bromley, Kent BR1 1NA

ACKNOWLEDGEMENTS
The Author and Publishers are grateful to the following individuals and
companies for permission to reproduce copyright illustrations in this book:
The American Museum of Natural History: Neg. no. 322742, p. 30, Neg.
no. 322747, p. 35; AP/Wide World Photos: pp. 12, 37, 43, 48, 50, 51, 55,
67, 69, 70, 73, 75, 77, 78-79, 82, 84, 86, 89, 98, 99, 104-5, 107; Library of
Congress: p. 25; The Library of the Academy of Natural Sciences of
Philadelphia: pp. 20, 26, 29, 32, 34, 53, 59, 60; The National Archives: p. 92;
The Newark Museum: Photos by C. Suydam Cutting, #M76-C, c. 1935, p. 23,
#M19-C, c. 1935, p. 28, #I79-C, c. 1937, p. 46, Photo by Ewing Galloway,
#I22-G, c. 1910-12, p. 17, Photo by Dr. Roderick A. MacLeod, #P-5, p. 61;
Popperfoto: pp. 2, 80, 94; Reuters/Bettmann Newsphotos: pp. 87, 101, 102,
106; H. E. Richardson and the Trustees of the British Museum: pp. 22, 27;
Royal Geographical Society, London: pp. 14-15, 18, 33, 39; United Nations:
p. 93; UPI/Bettmann Newsphotos: pp. 44, 47, 52, 56, 63, 64-65, 74, 90, 96.

ISBN 0 245-60104-X Hardback
ISBN 0 245-60105-8 Paperback

Printed in Great Britain by The Bath Press

CONTENTS

WORLD LEADERS   PAST AND PRESENT

KONRAD ADENAUER
ALEXANDER THE GREAT
MARK ANTONY
KING ARTHUR
KEMAL ATATÜRK
CLEMENT ATTLEE
MENACHEM BEGIN
DAVID BEN GURION
BISMARCK
LÉON BLUM
SÍMON BOLÍVAR
CESARE BORGIA
WILLY BRANDT
LEONID BREZHNEV
JULIUS CAESAR
CALVIN
FIDEL CASTRO
CATHERINE THE GREAT
CHARLEMAGNE
CHIANG KAI-SHEK
CHOU EN-LAI
WINSTON CHURCHILL
CLEMENCEAU
CLEOPATRA
CORTES
OLIVER CROMWELL
DANTON
CHARLES DE GAULLE
DE VALERA
DISRAELI
DWIGHT D. EISENHOWER
ELEANOR OF AQUITAINE
QUEEN ELIZABETH I
FERDINAND AND ISABELLA

FRANCO
FREDERICK THE GREAT
INDIRA GANDHI
MOHANDAS K. GANDHI
GARIBALDI
GENGHIS KHAN
GLADSTONE
DAG HAMMARSKJÖLD
HENRY VIII
HENRY OF NAVARRE
HINDENBURG
ADOLF HITLER
HO CHI MINH
KING HUSSEIN
IVAN THE TERRIBLE
ANDREW JACKSON
THOMAS JEFFERSON
JOAN OF ARC
POPE JOHN XXIII
LYNDON JOHNSON
BENITO JUÁREZ
JOHN F. KENNEDY
JOMO KENYATTA
AYATOLLAH KHOMEINI
NIKITA KHRUSHCHEV
MARTIN LUTHER KING
HENRY KISSINGER
VLADIMIR LENIN
ABRAHAM LINCOLN
LLOYD GEORGE
LOUIS XIV
MARTIN LUTHER
JUDAS MACCABEUS
MAO TSE TUNG

MARY, QUEEN OF SCOTS
GOLDA MEIR
METTERNICH
BENITO MUSSOLINI
NAPOLEON
JAMAL NASSER
JAWALHARLAL NEHRU
NERO
NICHOLAS II
RICHARD NIXON
KWAME NKRUMAH
PERICLES
JUAN PERÓN
MUAMMAR QADDAFI
ROBESPIERRE
ELEANOR ROOSEVELT
FRANKLIN D. ROOSEVELT
ANWAR SADAT
SUN YAT-SEN
JOSEPH STALIN
TAMERLANE
TENZIN GYATSO THE DALAI LAMA
MOTHER TERESA
MARGARET THATCHER
IOSIF TITO
LEON TROTSKY
PIERRE TRUDEAU
HARRY S. TRUMAN
QUEEN VICTORIA
GEORGE WASHINGTON
CHAIM WEIZMANN
WOODROW WILSON
XERXES

ON LEADERSHIP

Arthur M. Schlesinger, jr.

LEADERSHIP, it may be said, is really what makes the world go round. Love no doubt smooths the passage; but love is a private transaction between consenting adults. Leadership is a public transaction with history. The idea of leadership affirms the capacity of individuals to move, inspire, and mobilize masses of people so that they act together in pursuit of an end. Sometimes leadership serves good purposes, sometimes bad; but whether the end is benign or evil, great leaders are those men and women who leave their personal stamp on history.

Now, the very concept of leadership implies the proposition that individuals can make a difference. This proposition has never been universally accepted. From classical times to the present day, eminent thinkers have regarded individuals as no more than the agents and pawns of larger forces, whether the gods and goddesses of the ancient world or, in the modern era, race, class, nation, the dialectic, the will of the people, the spirit of the times, history itself. Against such forces, the individual dwindles into insignificance.

So contends the thesis of historical determinism. Tolstoy's great novel *War and Peace* offers a famous statement of the case. Why, Tolstoy asked, did millions of men in the Napoleonic Wars, denying their human feelings and their common sense, move back and forth across Europe slaughtering their fellows? "The war," Tolstoy answered, "was bound to happen simply because it was bound to happen." All prior history predetermined it. As for leaders, they, Tolstoy said, "are but the labels that serve to give a name to an end and, like labels, they have the least possible connection with the event." The greater the leader, "the more conspicuous the inevitability and the predestination of every act he commits." The leader, said Tolstoy, is "the slave of history."

Determinism takes many forms. Marxism is the determinism of class. Nazism the determinism of race. But the idea of men and women as the slaves of history runs athwart the deepest human instincts. Rigid determinism abolishes the idea of human freedom—the assumption of free choice that underlies every move we make, every word we speak, every thought we think. It abolishes the idea of human responsibility, since it is manifestly unfair to reward or punish people for actions that are by definition beyond their control. No one can live consistently by any deterministic creed. The Marxist states prove this themselves by their extreme susceptibility to the cult of leadership.

More than that, history refutes the idea that individuals make no difference. In December 1931 a British politician crossing Park Avenue in New York City between 76th and 77th Streets around ten-thirty at night looked in the wrong direction and was knocked down by an automobile—a moment, he later recalled, of a man aghast, a world aglare: "I do not understand why I was not broken like an eggshell or squashed like a gooseberry." Fourteen months later an American politician, sitting in an open car in Miami, Florida, was fired on by an assassin; the man beside him was hit. Those who believe that individuals make no difference to history might well ponder whether the next two decades would have been the same had Mario Constasino's car killed Winston Churchill in 1931 and Giuseppe Zangara's bullet killed Franklin Roosevelt in 1933. Suppose, in addition, that Adolf Hitler had been killed in the street fighting during the Munich *Putsch* of 1923 and that Lenin had died of typhus during World War I. What would the 20th century be like now?

For better or for worse, individuals do make a difference. "The notion that a people can run itself and its affairs anonymously," wrote the philosopher William James, "is now well known to be the silliest of absurdities. Mankind does nothing save through initiatives on the part of inventors, great or small, and imitation by the rest of us—these are the sole factors in human progress. Individuals of genius show the way, and set the patterns, which common people then adopt and follow."

Leadership, James suggests, means leadership in thought as well as in action. In the long run, leaders in thought may well make the greater difference to the world. But, as Woodrow Wilson once said, "Those only are leaders of men, in the general eye, who lead in action. . . . It is at their hands that new thought gets its translation into the crude language of deeds." Leaders in thought often invent in solitude and obscurity, leaving to later generations the tasks of imitation. Leaders in action—the leaders portrayed in this series—have to be effective in their own time.

And they cannot be effective by themselves. They must act in response to the rhythms of their age. Their genius must be adapted, in a phrase of William James's, "to the receptivities of the moment." Leaders are useless without followers. "There goes the mob," said the French politician hearing a clamour in the streets. "I am their leader. I must follow them." Great leaders turn the inchoate emotions of the mob to purposes of their own.

They seize on the opportunities of their time, the hopes, fears, frustrations, crises, potentialities. They succeed when events have prepared the way for them, when the community is awaiting to be aroused, when they can provide the clarifying and organizing ideas. Leadership ignites the circuit between the individual and the mass and thereby alters history.

It may alter history for better or for worse. Leaders have been responsible for the most extravagant follies and most monstrous crimes that have beset suffering humanity. They have also been vital in such gains as humanity has made in individual freedom, religious and racial tolerance, social justice, and respect for human rights.

There is no sure way to tell in advance who is going to lead for good and who for evil. But a glance at the gallery of men and women in *World Leaders—Past and Present* suggests some useful tests.

One test is this: Do leaders lead by force or by persuasion? By command or by consent? Through most of history leadership was exercised by the divine right of authority. The duty of followers was to defer and to obey. "Theirs not to reason why / Theirs but to do and die." On occasion, as with the so-called enlightened despots of the 18th century in Europe, absolutist leadership was animated by humane purposes. More often, absolutism nourished the passion for domination, land, gold, and conquest and resulted in tyranny.

The great revolution of modern times has been the revolution of equality. The idea that all people should be equal in their legal condition has undermined the old structure of authority, hierarchy, and deference. The revolution of equality has had two contrary effects on the nature of leadership. For equality, as Alexis de Tocqueville pointed out in his great study *Democracy in America*, might mean equality in servitude as well as equality in freedom.

"I know of only two methods of establishing equality in the political world," Tocqueville wrote. "Rights must be given to every citizen, or none at all to anyone . . . save one, who is the master of all." There was no middle ground "between the sovereignty of all and the absolute power of one man." In his astonishing prediction of 20th-century totalitarian dictatorship, Tocqueville explained how the revolution of equality could lead to the *"Führerprinzip"* and more terrible absolutism than the world had ever known.

But when rights are given to every citizen and the sovereignty of all is established, the problem of leadership takes a new form, becomes more exacting than ever before. It is easy to issue commands and enforce them by the rope and the stake, the concentration camp and the *gulag.* It is much harder to use argument and achievement to overcome opposition and win consent. The Founding Fathers of the United States understood the difficulty. They believed that history had given them the opportunity to decide, as Alexander Hamilton wrote in the first Federalist Paper, whether men are indeed capable of basing government on "reflection and choice, or whether they are forever destined to depend . . . on accident and force."

Government by reflection and choice called for a new style of leadership and a new quality of followership. It required leaders to be responsive to popular concerns, and it required followers to be active and informed participants in the process. Democracy does not eliminate emotion from politics; sometimes it fosters demagoguery; but it is confident that, as the greatest of democratic leaders put it, you cannot fool all of the people all of the time. It measures leadership by results and retires those who overreach or falter or fail.

It is true that in the long run despots are measured by results too. But they can postpone the day of judgment, sometimes indefinitely, and in the meantime they can do infinite harm. It is also true that democracy is no guarantee of virtue and intelligence in government, for the voice of the people is not necessarily the voice of God. But democracy, by assuring the right of opposition, offers built-in resistance to the evils inherent in absolutism. As the theologian Reinhold Niebuhr summed it up, "Man's capacity for justice makes democracy possible, but man's inclination to injustice makes democracy necessary."

A second test for leadership is the end for which power is sought. When leaders have as their goal the supremacy of a master race or the promotion of totalitarian revolution or the acquisition and exploitation of colonies or the protection of greed and privilege or the preservation of personal power, it is likely that their leadership will do little to advance the cause of humanity. When their goal is the abolition of slavery, the liberation of women, the enlargement of opportunity for the poor and powerless, the extension of equal rights to racial minorities, the defence of the freedoms of expression and opposition, it is likely that their leadership will increase the sum of human liberty and welfare.

Leaders have done great harm to the world. They have also conferred great benefits. You will find both sorts in this series. Even "good" leaders must be regarded with a certain wariness.

Leaders are not demigods; they put on their trousers one leg after another just like ordinary mortals. No leader is infallible, and every leader needs to be reminded of this at regular intervals. Irreverence irritates leaders but is their salvation. Unquestioning submission corrupts leaders and demeans followers. Making a cult of a leader is always a mistake. Fortunately hero worship generates its own antidote. "Every hero," said Emerson, "becomes a bore at last."

The signal benefit the great leaders confer is to embolden the rest of us to live according to our own best selves, to be active, insistent, and resolute in affirming our own sense of things. For great leaders attest to the reality of human freedom against the supposed inevitabilities of history. And they attest to the wisdom and power that may lie within the most unlikely of us, which is why Abraham Lincoln remains the supreme example of great leadership. A great leader, said Emerson, exhibits new possibilities to all humanity. "We feed on genius. . . . Great men exist that there may be greater men."

Great leaders, in short, justify themselves by emancipating and empowering their followers. So humanity struggles to master its destiny, remembering with Alexis de Tocqueville: "It is true that around every man a fatal circle is traced beyond which he cannot pass; but within the wide verge of that circle he is powerful and free; as it is with man, so with communities."

1

The Searchers

On a winter afternoon in 1937, a small group of travellers rode into the village of Taktser in the hills of China's remote western province of Tsinghai. As the riders reined in their horses in the courtyard of a modest farmhouse, their leader introduced himself to the woman of the house as an itinerant merchant and asked her permission to use her cooking fire to brew some tea for his companions. He addressed her in Tibetan, the language of the country that lay hundreds of miles to the southwest.

It was not an unusual request for a traveller in this part of the world to make, and the woman, answering in Tibetan, hospitably agreed. But what she did not know was that her guests were anything but common traders. Their leader was in fact a top official of the Tibetan government, and the man who seemed to be the travellers' servant was actually Kwetsang Rinpoche, a high-ranking lama, or monk, from the great and distant Buddhist monastery of Sera. Nor was it by chance that they had stopped at this particular house in Taktser. For Kwetsang Rinpoche and his companions were a search party,

He [the Dalai Lama] is the rebirth of the historical figure he was in his preceding life, a link in a chain that starts in history and leads back through legend to a deity in ancient times.
—R. A. STEIN
French historian

Tenzin Gyatso, the 14th Dalai Lama of Tibet, at the age of five in 1940. Born to a peasant family in a distant and remote region, he was chosen in 1937 by a search party composed of Tibet's highest religious and government figures, who believed him to be a reincarnation of the 13 previous Dalai Lamas.

The village of Taktser, birthplace of the 14th Dalai Lama. Populated by Tibetans, Taktser is located on a caravan route in the western Chinese province of Tsinghai, some 700 miles from the heart of Tibet. A Buddhist monastery overlooks the village.

and their mission in this tiny Tibetan village in a far-off Chinese province was to find the reincarnation of Tibet's god-king, the Dalai Lama.

It had been three years since the death of Thubten Gyatso, 13th in the line of Dalai Lamas, and since that time a search had been on for the male child in whom the spirit of the ruler would be reborn. When Thubten Gyatso died, his body had been found facing northeast, and as the search progressed in that direction from village to village other signs indicated that the reincarnation would be

found in Tsinghai, known to the Tibetans as Amdo.
When Kwetsang Rinpoche and his companions arrived in that remote region they heard reports that
a young boy in the village of Taktser was worth in-
vestigating. He was born, they were told, on the fifth
day of the fifth month of the Wood Hog Year of the
16th cycle of the Tibetan calendar, and he now lived
in a peasant's house that stood in the shadow of a
hilltop monastery. It was in that very house that the
search party now sat, warming their hands and
brewing tea by the cooking fire.

Before long the child they had come to see appeared. He was an inquisitive two-year-old named Lhamo Dhondrub, and the first thing he did was to climb onto the lap of Kwetsang Rinpoche and begin playing with a rosary that hung around the lama's neck. The necklace, insisted the little boy, was his. The strangers' hopes were immediately raised; the rosary had in fact belonged to the 13th Dalai Lama. Kwetsang Rinpoche told young Lhamo that he would give him the rosary, but only if the child knew who Kwetsang Rinpoche was. The travellers listened in amazement as Lhamo promptly replied that he was a lama of Sera, and then proceeded to identify the other three men, two of them by name. The searchers, however, betrayed no sign of their astonishment. They thanked the woman for the tea, packed up their things, mounted their horses, and moved on. But they would be back.

Sensing that they might have located the 14th incarnation of the Dalai Lama, the search party returned to Taktser with more monks a few days later to conduct an official examination of the child. Now it was clear to the boy's parents just who the travellers of a few days before really were.

Lhamo was brought before the monks, and the examination began. They showed the child a number of objects, some of which had belonged to the 13th Dalai Lama, the rest of which were replicas or similar objects with no connection to the late ruler. Lhamo was asked which ones were the Dalai Lama's. The boy did not hesitate; without fail, he chose only the Dalai Lama's possessions. The investigators were astounded but not yet convinced. They offered the child two walking sticks, one of which had been the Dalai Lama's; the other had once been used by him but had later been given away to someone else. Lhamo walked over to the stick that had been given away, grasped it, and put it down. He then moved over to the true staff of the Dalai Lama and picked it up with both hands.

Still the monks were not convinced. They inspected Lhamo for a number of bodily marks traditionally associated with the Dalai Lamas: large ears, eyebrows curving up at their ends, streaks like

Despite the mystique with which some westerners like to regard the whole process of selecting lamas, the custom was clearly adopted and maintained primarily for reasons of statecraft.
—DAVID SNELLGORVE &
  HUGH RICHARDSON
  English historians

tiger skin on the legs, moles in certain locations on the torso, a palm print resembling a conch shell. The marks were all there.

That was enough; the examiners were satisfied that they were truly in the presence of the 14th Dalai Lama. Some of the investigators broke down and cried. As far as they were concerned, the little two-year-old was no longer Lhamo Dhondrub, the son of a peasant. He was now the religious and secular leader of Tibet. He was the Dalai Lama, a sacred being.

Now the boy would be taken on a long journey over the foothills and through the valleys of some of the highest mountain ranges in the world, to Lhasa, Tibet's capital and largest city, where he would be enthroned and shown to the people of the nation.

The 13th Dalai Lama, Thubten Gyatso, who died in 1933 after a reign of 58 years. The Dalai Lama, the supreme figure of Tibetan Buddhism and the Tibetan state, was revered as a living god-king in the devoutly religious nation. When the 13th Dalai Lama died facing northeast, those searching for his reincarnation headed in that direction for Tsinghai.

A 1915 photo of coal carriers in Amdo, the Tibetan name for China's Tsinghai province. A region of mountains, high plateaus, swamps, and deserts, Amdo was thinly populated by Tibetans, Mongols, Chinese, and Turkic peoples. Horses and camels were the sole means of transport there until the 1950s, when the first motor roads were finally built.

But news of the discovery of the 14th Dalai Lama had already reached Ma Bufeng, the Chinese warlord who controlled much of Tsinghai province. Before the travelling party could get under way, Ma sent word that unless the Tibetans paid him a large sum of money, he would not allow the boy to leave his territory. As a Muslim, the warlord had no regard for the Buddhist institution of the Dalai Lama, and he knew that the Tibetan government would be willing to pay a high price for the child's safety. After months of negotiations that left Ma richer by 40,000 Chinese silver dollars and in possession of a full set of the 13th Dalai Lama's robes and ornaments as well as a gold-lettered set of Buddhist scriptures, the warlord finally gave his permission to let the boy proceed.

Young Lhamo Dhondrub, his parents, his four brothers and sisters, and his escort of lamas and Tibetan government officials set out on the 100-day journey to Lhasa in the late summer of 1939. At first, they travelled southwest with a caravan of Muslim traders over the hilly grasslands of central Tsinghai, then they moved up into the mountain passes of the towering Kunlun Shan range. They rode past glaciers and beneath snowcapped mountain peaks soaring more than 20,000 feet into the clear blue sky. Skirting icy lakes and crossing roaring rivers, they finally reached the border of Tibet, where they were joined by a cavalry detachment of the Tibetan army. They had gone more than 400 miles, a little more than halfway to Lhasa.

They followed the caravan track as it climbed high into the Thangla Ri range, past more lakes and glaciers, down into valleys, then up again across the Nyanchen Thangla range. Now they passed villages and monasteries more frequently, and on a high mountain road they were met by representatives of the Kshag (the council of government ministers who advised the Dalai Lama on secular matters) and the Tsongdu (the national assembly, made up of aristocrats and lamas from each of Tibet's regions). On the final days of the journey, as they descended the southern slopes of the Nyenchen Thangla, Lhamo rode in a golden litter carried on the shoulders of his retainers. He was preceded by a long line of monks in tall headdresses, announcing his approach by sounding 10-foot-long horns that sent a single, low note echoing for miles through the lonely valleys and past the towering mountains.

Finally, on October 6, 1939, the travellers came within sight of Lhasa. In the distance the city looked like a jumble of low buildings punctuated by the towers of shrines and temples, but that was not what caught the travellers' eyes. Perched atop a long ridge that loomed over the city was an enormous building: the gigantic Potala palace. At 13 stories in height, with more than 1,000 rooms contained within its walls of solid masonry built several yards thick, it was one of the largest and most spectacular buildings in the world. And it was to be Lhamo Dhondrub's new home.

The original intention was that the Dalai Lama himself should be the religious ruler, as his nature was supposed to be eminently spiritual, and that he should have a regent to conduct the administration with the Khan himself as overall protector, ready to step in whenever there was need.
—DAVID SNELLGROVE & HUGH RICHARDSON English historians

2

The Compassionate Spirit of the Mountains

When the procession bearing Lhamo Dhondrup entered Lhasa on the afternoon of October 6, 1939, the young Dalai Lama was carried to a silk tent at the base of the Potala. There he sat for the next two days, blessing thousands of his new subjects as they filed past him in reverence and awe.

Lhasa, a city of some 70,000 people with massive official and religious buildings, row after row of 2-story houses, and bustling streets, must have seemed a world away from Taktser. At the centre of the city lay Tsuglakhang, the enormous religious complex that contained Tibet's holiest shrine, the Jokhang Cathedral. Tsuglakhang was encircled by Lhasa's busiest street and marketplace, the Barkhor, where crowds of shoppers and worshippers from all over Tibet converged every day. Ragged beggars mingled with haughty aristocrats, prosperous nomad women paraded their wealth by wearing discs of silver in their hair, and street performers and shopkeepers did their best to relieve passers-by of some of their money.

[Lamaism] is a whole world, immensely complex, embracing many aspects: a rich and subtle philosophy . . . a very advanced depth psychology linked to techniques of meditation and the control of psycho-physiological functions (yoga); an enormous pantheon; countless rituals; popular practices; cosmological speculations; systems of divinations.
—R. A. STEIN
French historian,
on Lamaism

The seven-year-old Dalai Lama in 1942, three years after he was brought to Tibet and installed as its king. The swastikas on the tapestry at the base of his throne are an ancient good-luck symbol in Tibet, India, and the rest of south Asia.

The retinue bringing the young Dalai Lama arrives in the Tibetan capital, Lhasa, in 1939. The caravan that carried the 3-year-old spent 100 days covering the 700 miles between Taktser and Lhasa, crossing huge mountain ranges, vast prairies, raging rivers, and lands controlled by warlords and bandits.

Shortly after the Tibetan new year, the Barkhor would literally overflow with people, as pilgrims flooded into Lhasa for the great festival known as Monlam Chenmo. Beyond Barkhor lay another circular road, the Lingkhor, which ran right around Lhasa. This street too, was commonly clogged with pilgrims, many of whom would regularly prostrate themselves as they slowly circled the city in an act of religious devotion. Lhasa was clearly a very sacred place to the Tibetans; it was, after all, the home of the Dalai Lama.

Before Lhamo Dhondrub took his place in the royal quarters of the Potala, he would have to give up his name and take a new one more suitable for a Dalai Lama, a Mongolian term which translates literally to "Ocean Lama," a Buddhist way of expressing the all-encompassing wisdom of the spiritual leader.

Accordingly, the boy was given a long string of honorific titles and names: Jetsun Jamphel Ngawang Lobsang Yeshi Tenzin Gyatso Sisunwangyur Tshunpa Getson Mapal Dhepal Sango, which translates roughly to Gentle Glory, Holy Lord, Eloquent, Compassionate, Ocean of Wisdom, Pure in Mind, Learned Defender of the Faith. With his complete name reserved for ceremonial occasions, the 14th Dalai Lama would commonly be known by a shortened version: Tenzin (Holder of Faith) Gyatso (Ocean of Wisdom).

Now Tenzin Gyatso was ready to be installed in the Potala, a ceremony that took place on February 22, 1940. Sitting on the Lion Throne in the gigantic hilltop palace, the seven-year-old boy literally towered over his subjects. In the city below, and throughout Tibet, he was regarded not only as the incarnation of the 13 previous leaders of the Gelugpa order, the dominant sect of Tibetan Buddhism, but also as the incarnation of Chenrezi, a being whose goodness long ago enabled him to escape the eternal cycle of birth, death, and rebirth to which Buddhists believe all creatures are subject.

According to Buddhist teachings, all beings are locked into the birth-death-rebirth cycle, known as *samsara* in Sanskrit, the ancient language of India. During a being's series of lives, he, she, or it

The Potala on the hill above Lhasa, a 1,000-room palace built by the fifth Dalai Lama between 1645 and 1694, housed the Tibetan government and was the winter residence of the Dalai Lama. Before being installed there, the young king was given a series of names and titles, including Tenzin (Holder of Faith) Gyatso (Ocean of Wisdom), by which he is now commonly known.

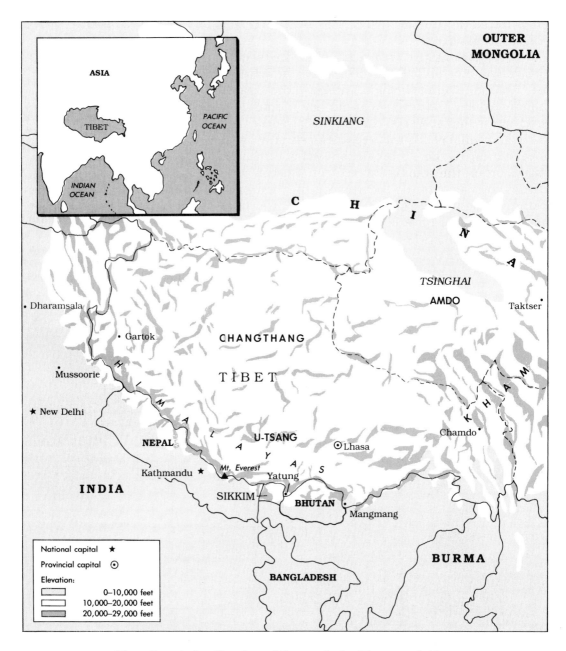

More than twice the size of France but with a population
of just 2 million, Tibet is the world's most mountainous country. In the 1200s, 600 years after the introduction of Buddhism into Tibet, the country came under the
control of the Mongols; in 1578 the Mongol overlords originated the institution of the Dalai Lama.

generates a force called *karma*, in which the sins or virtues of one life are punished or rewarded in the subsequent life. Some beings, by performing enough good deeds and living virtuous enough lives during their various incarnations, accumulate enough "good karma" to escape the birth-death-re-birth cycle. They then reach a sort of paradise called *nirvana*, a state of total enlightenment in which all desire, suffering, and individual consciousness disappears. It is the goal of every devout Buddhist to attain nirvana.

According to Buddhist belief, however, the goodness of some beings is so complete, so perfect, that they choose not to enter nirvana. Out of compassion, these beings choose instead to return to earth to be reborn, so that they may provide guidance to

A portion of the Barkhor, Lhasa's main market street, with Buddhist prayer flags flying atop the houses. In 1939, Lhasa had a population of about 70,000, making it the nation's largest city; during religious festivals thousands more would pour into Lhasa from all over the country.

Reting monastery, founded in 1057. As much as 20 percent of the country's population lived in 2,700 monasteries and nunneries throughout Tibet. The larger ones, such as Reting and the 3 great monasteries near Lhasa (Drepung, Sera, and Ganden) had as many as 10,000 residents each and owned vast tracts of land.

others. In Sanskrit, such a being is called a *bodhisattva*, and the bodhisattva named Avalokitesvara (the Compassionate Spirit of the Mountains) is regarded as the most supremely compassionate of all. In Tibetan, Avalokitesvara is known as Chenrezi, and Tibetans believe that the Dalai Lama is Chenrezi's reincarnation.

The Dalai Lama's significance was not confined solely to spiritual matters; it extended to the material world of politics as well. Like eight of the Dalai Lamas before him, young Tenzin Gyatso was to become the absolute ruler of one of the most remote and isolated countries in the world.

Outside the palace gates of the Potala lay the vast and wild land of Tenzin Gyatso's subjects, less than 2.5 million people scattered over 500,000 square miles of territory known to them as the Land of Snows. Tibet is surrounded by the tallest mountain ranges on earth — the Himalayas, Karakoram, Kunlun, Min Shan, and Ta-Hsueh Shan — which throughout history have isolated it from the rest of the world. The mountain ranges meander into and throughout Tibet, making travel and communication within the country difficult as well.

The northern half of Tibet is a windswept mountain wilderness, populated only by wild animals and an occasional band of nomadic hunters. Just to the south of this wilderness region is a relatively thin strip of land — a mixture of mountains, plateaus, and lakes — inhabited by nomadic herders of yaks and goats. At the mountainous western end of this strip of pastureland, along the border with Nepal and northernmost India, rise the headwaters of the Indus and the Ganges, two of the great rivers of south Asia; in the mountains at the eastern end lie the sources of the Brahmaputra, the Salween, the Mekong, and the Yangtze, four of east Asia's great rivers. Most of eastern Tibet is encompassed by Kham province, inhabited by the Khampas, a people widely regarded as wild and dangerous by other Tibetans.

In the centre of Tibet lies the vast Changthang plain, an area of salt flats not unlike those of Utah, but situated at an altitude of 15,000 feet. These give way to the valleys and rolling pasturelands of south-central Tibet, home to most of the country's population. Lhasa is located in this region, which is also dotted with towns, villages, monasteries, and nunneries. In 1939, as it had been for centuries, this was also the home of Tibet's farmlands, where wheat and barley were grown, as well as peaches, apricots, grapes, and rice. Harvests yielded more than enough to feed the small population; while famine was often a problem throughout most of Asia, in Tibet it was virtually unknown.

Tenzin Gyatso was the second youngest of the five children in his family. In this photo taken in Lhasa in 1946 are, from left to right, his brothers Taktser Rinpoche and Gyalo Thondup, his father Chokyong Tsering, his mother Sonam Isamo, and his brother Ngari Rinpoche.

This was the Dalai Lama's immense domain, but even outside Tibet the Dalai Lama could claim some loose, largely spiritual authority in a number of neighbouring lands. To the southeast, in the foothills of the Himalayas, lay the independent kingdom of Bhutan, whose people followed the religion of the Gelugpa and recognized the Dalai Lama as their head. The same applied to the nearby kingdom of Sikkim, the principality of Ladakh in India, and the province of Mustang in the Himalayan kingdom of Nepal; all of these lands were religiously and culturally tied to Tibet and the authority of the Dalai Lama. To the northeast, there was the region where he was born, Amdo, which had been a Tibetan province until 1724; tens of thousands of Tibetans and Mongolians lived there and adhered to Tibetan Buddhism.

Finally, the still more distant northeastern lands of Mongolia — divided into Inner Mongolia (a province of China's) and Outer Mongolia (an independent nation) — were also traditional strongholds of Gelugpa Buddhism. In the 1920s, however, a revolution in Outer Mongolia transformed that nation into a Communist republic, like the Soviet Union. Outer Mongolia's Communist government, believing that religion was a means of oppressing the people, dismantled the institution of Gelugpa Buddhism there. It confiscated monasteries and redistributed their enormous landholdings to the people.

Norbulingka (Jewel Park), the Dalai Lama's summer residence just outside Lhasa. Far less severe than the enormous, fortresslike Potala, Norbulingka was famed for the peacocks and deer that roamed its gardens.

The majority of Outer Mongolia's lamas, who comprised as much as one-third of that nation's male population, were forced to return to secular life.

Mongolia's experience carried the first warnings of what Tibet would face in the years to come. Tenzin Gyatso's predecessor, the 13th Dalai Lama — "the Great 13th," as he was known in Tibet — had noticed the gathering storm in the outside world that would one day threaten his kingdom. As he began the final year of his reign in 1932, the Great 13th wrote his last testament to his subjects and his successor. In it he predicted that unless efforts were made to strengthen Tibet, the day would come "when our political system . . . will be reduced to an empty name, my officials deprived of their power, and their property will be subjugated like slaves by the enemy. My people, subjected to fear and misery, will be unable to endure day or night. Such an era will surely come!"

Such dire prophecies could have meant little to the four-year-old Tenzin Gyatso, and it would be quite some time before he would be called upon to deal with such matters. In the meantime, his kingdom was being run by regents who would have effective control until the Dalai Lama reached adulthood.

Tenzin Gyatso began his life in the Potala in splendid isolation from the everyday world of his subjects. Even his own family would not be permitted to share his palace; new lodgings were built for them just below the Potala's walls. And although he met with his parents and brothers regularly, for the most part Tenzin Gyatso would now live in the company of the elderly monks who would tutor and raise him.

In the summer months he would leave Lhasa, accompanied by his court and family, for Norbulingka, a palace complex just outside the city's western perimeter. Within the walls of the Norbulingka were a number of small palaces and temples — as well as extensive gardens filled with birds and tame animals, such as peacocks, pheasants, and musk deer. By all accounts, it was in these pleasant surroundings that the young Dalai Lama spent his happiest times, a child revered as a living god.

Chortens, or Buddhist shrines, on a remote Tibetan mountainside. Tibetan Buddhism was widely practised within and beyond Tibet's borders, giving the Dalai Lama spiritual authority over hundreds of thousands of believers in Mongolia, Nepal, Bhutan, Sikkim, and portions of western China.

3

The Perfection of Wisdom

As Tenzin Gyatso settled down to his first years in Lhasa, his mountain kingdom seemed secure in its isolation from the world war that was engulfing Asia and Europe. Surrounded in the immense Potala by monks and the complex rituals of the Gelugpa order, Tenzin Gyatso's life had little in common with that of other leaders.

Both the Dalai Lama and his land were very much in the hands of the Gelugpa establishment. The regent (the chief adviser and the man who would rule in the name of the Dalai Lama until Tenzin Gyatso reached adulthood) was himself a high lama, revered as the reincarnation of one of Tibet's Buddhist saints. One of the four members of the Kshag was also a Gelugpa monk. Below the Kshag were two government departments, one of which, the secretariat, was composed entirely of lamas.

According to Buddhist tradition, service to others is one of the most important religious practices. So long as my motivation is correct, my temporal work is an act of religion.
—TENZIN GYATSO
THE DALAI LAMA

A Tibetan banner depicting Siddhārtha Gautama (the 6th century B.C. Indian mystic known as the Buddha) and scenes from his former lives. Buddhism came to Tibet in the 7th century A.D., blended with the local religion of spirit worship, and came to permeate every aspect of Tibetan life. By 1940, Tibet was often called the world's last theocracy.

A lama, or Buddhist monk, stands behind a group of young novices at a Tibetan monastery. Tenzin Gyatso underwent the same educational and religious training given to Tibetan boys whose families enrolled them in the monkhood. In addition, the young Dalai Lama learned to read and write in all four forms of Tibetan script.

The other major component of the government, the Tsongdu, was a "national assembly" but in no way a parliament in the traditional sense. Its members — all of them heads of monasteries or leading noblemen — were not elected but appointed by the Dalai Lama, the regent, or the ministers of the Kshag. They could only convene when summoned to Lhasa, and even then their sole task was to approve the specific plans placed before them by the Kshag. The Kshag and secretariat also functioned as the nation's highest court of law, deciding which local official would act as judge in an important case. A condemned defendant had the right to appeal to the Dalai Lama himself, but punishment tended to be severe if he or she were found guilty at any level of the judicial process.

The government's primary expense was the up-keep of the large Gelugpa monasteries, which included not only building maintenance but also free breakfasts served daily to thousands of monks and the purchase of butter, used as wax, to light the millions of candles in the monasteries. To pay for all this, the government levied taxes on other monasteries and the large private estates, which in turn taxed tenant farmers; money was rare in Tibet, so most taxes were paid in grain, oil, meat, and butter. The individual who owned the most land in Tibet was the Dalai Lama himself, and his private treasury, inherited from all the previous Dalai Lamas, was enormous, filling room after room in the Potala with gold, silver, precious gems, silks, carpets, and religious artifacts.

The kingdom that Tenzin Gyatso was being groomed to rule was a theocracy, a state run by religious figures according to religious doctrine. Indeed, the Gelugpa order was much more than an order of monks that owned land and ran the country; it actually comprised a large portion of the Tibetan people — as much as 10 percent of Tibet's population during Tenzin Gyatso's reign, according

A group of lamas of the Gelugpa order. Although there are scores of different orders in Tibetan Buddhism, the Gelugpa has predominated since the mid-1600s, 250 years after it was founded. All 14 Dalai Lamas belonged to the Gelugpa (also known as the Yellow Hats), and the order ran the Tibetan government.

to some estimates. Of the 2,700 monasteries in Tibet, scores belonged to the Gelugpa, and the order's largest monasteries — Sera, Ganden, and Drepung — were all in the vicinity of Lhasa. The monasteries looked more like fortress towns than religious institutions; Drepung alone was populated by some 10,000 lamas.

Such prodigious numbers were only possible because Tibetan families, from the poorest to the richest, would commonly send one of their children to a monastery to be raised from an early age. Because the monasteries owned much of Tibet's agricultural land, which they would rent to common farmers or herders, a family would sometimes give a boy to the monkhood in place of the taxes or debts it owed to a particular monastery. The wealth of the large monasteries made the day-to-day life of a monk easier than that of an ordinary Tibetan farmer or herder. The monastery was also the only place where a child could acquire an education, another reason for giving him or her to the monkhood or nunhood. But whatever material reasons a family might have had for sending a child to the lamas, spiritual reasons remained paramount. Tibet was a land where religious belief pervaded every aspect of daily life; sending a child to a monastery was a sincere act of devotion on the part of any pious family.

Two masked lamas perform a ritual dance. Many aspects of Bon — the ancient Tibetan religion of spirit worship — were adopted by Tibetan Buddhism, including the veneration of hundreds of deities; the practise of "sky burial" (freeing the souls of the dead by leaving their bodies on hilltops to be devoured by vultures); and the honouring of Tibet's ruler as divine.

A Tibetan depiction of the god Hayagriva, the protector of horses, one of many Bon deities incorporated into Tibetan Buddhism. Buddhists believe that all outward reality is an illusion and that through devotion and goodness a being can be liberated from the suffering of birth, death, and rebirth and achieve total enlightenment.

The power and privileges of the Gelugpa order had ancient roots in the history of Tibet and Tibetan Buddhism. Buddhism was introduced to Tibet by Indian monks in the 7th century A.D., more than 1,000 years after it had been founded by Siddhārtha Gautama, an Indian mystic and philosopher who is known simply as the Buddha. His philosophy was an outgrowth of the Hindu religion, then as now the predominant faith in India.

Originally, the Buddhist religion taught that individuals should seek spiritual enlightenment for their own sake, but as Buddhism grew, developed, and took on many of the features of other local religions, a new sect emerged. Called Mahayana ("the Greater Way") Buddhism, the new sect placed much more emphasis on compassion for all living creatures. Mahayana Buddhism taught that enlightenment should be achieved for the sake of liberating all beings from the sorrows of their existence.

The Mahayana quickly became the dominant sect, displacing the old sect (which came to be called Hinayana, or "the Lesser Way") at about the time Buddhism first entered Tibet around A.D. 640 under the sponsorship of King Songsten Gampo and his two wives, one of whom was Chinese and the other Nepalese. During this period in the country's history, Tibet was ruled by warrior kings and was making its first contact with the Chinese empire to the east.

Mahayana and Hinayana existed side by side with the local Tibetan religion of spirit worship (later known as Bon) until 792, when a religious debate was held between the competing Buddhist sects. The Mahayana side was represented by an Indian scholar and the Hinayana by a Chinese scholar. The Indian scholar won, and from then on Mahayana Buddhism was the predominant form of Buddhism in Tibet.

Nevertheless, Buddhists would have an uphill struggle in Tibet for the next 150 years. Around the year 836 a nobleman named Lang Darma, who was fiercely opposed to the new religion, ascended the throne and immediately began to persecute Buddhists. Lang Darma was apparently an adherent to Bon, which had been steadily losing ground to Buddhism over the preceding decades. Bon belief held that the world was populated by hundreds of various good spirits and evil demons, who could be summoned for protection or warded off by performing the proper ceremonies; eventually its practice merged with so many Buddhist precepts that the two Tibetan religions became virtually indistinguishable from one another. In any event, Lang Darma's persecutions forced many Buddhists to retreat to remote parts of the country, where they established several monasteries to preserve their endangered religion. It was the first flowering of the Tibetan monastic tradition.

In 842 Lang Darma was assassinated by a Buddhist monk in a daring attack that is celebrated by Tibetans to this day. The assassination brought to an end the line of Tibetan kings and gave way to a long period in which the Buddhist monasteries were able to promote their religion and acquire political

One would hardly expect to find in this Asian society the modern Western notion of service to one's fellow men as a kind of social duty. But one can find enlightened self-interest, and this is often the more practical ideal.
—DAVID SNELLGROVE &
HUGH RICHARDSON
English historians

strength. By 1050, Tibet had become an entirely religious state no longer concerned with expanding its borders through warfare.

Because the monasteries had not developed under any central authority and were scattered over the vast land, it was inevitable that differences would arise between the various Buddhist establishments in Tibet. In time, many different sects were established, each of which sought to enhance its own power through political alliances against the other sects. The Gelugpa order, which eventually came to dominate Tibet's religious and political life, was among the sects involved in this struggle.

The Gelugpa order was established in the late 1300s by a lama known as Tsongkapa. Tsongkapa stressed a strict moral code for Gelugpa lamas, who, unlike monks in many other orders, were expected to observe celibacy and refrain from consuming intoxicants. In fact, Gelugpa means "those who follow virtue," but they came to be more commonly known as the Yellow Hats on account of their headgear, which distinguished them from other orders such as the "Red Hat" Kadampa and the "Black Hat" Karmapa.

Two lamas reading Tibetan religious texts. The body of Tibetan religious writing is enormous, much of it translations from the ancient Indian language of Sanskrit; the most famous in the West is *The Tibetan Book of the Dead*, a mystical text on reincarnation. Young Tenzin Gyatso studied hundreds of volumes of Tibetan religious literature.

The rigourous discipline of the Gelugpa lamas soon won Tsongkapa many followers, and from 1409 to 1419 three large monasteries were established for them: Ganden, Drepung, and Sera. All three were in the vicinity of Lhasa, which became the centre of the new order.

When Tsongkapa died in 1419, the Gelugpa appointed a successor and declared him to be a reincarnation of their founder. (The practise of locating the reincarnations of lamas had actually originated with the rival Karmapa sect, who regarded their leader as an incarnate bodhisattva.) The Gelugpa soon established an elabourate hierarchy of incarnate lamas of their own. Yet the impetus for the soon-to-be-established institution of the Dalai Lama would come not from Tibet but from Mongolia.

In the 44 years from 1183 until his death in 1227, Genghis Khan's Mongol armies swept across Asia, conquering and destroying everything in their path — from China in the east through central Asia and Mongolia in the centre to Persia in the west — en route to amassing the largest land empire in the history of the world. Tibet became part of that empire in 1207, when the leading Tibetan lamas submitted to Genghis Khan without resistance. Tibet was thus one of the few lands that escaped warfare and destruction at the hands of the Mongols. Nearly two centuries of Mongol overlordship ensued, and during that period the Mongols began to adopt Tibetan Buddhism.

In 1578, the chief of the western branch of the Mongols invited the Gelugpa's grand lama — who was the third incarnation of Tsongkapa — to become the Mongols' spiritual leader, an invitation the grand lama accepted. The Mongol chief bestowed the title Dalai Lama on the Gelugpa monk, and thus the institution was born. When the grand lama died 10 years later, the Gelugpa order found his reincarnation in the Mongol chief's great-grandson, who became the next Dalai Lama. This sealed the alliance between the Gelugpa and the Mongols.

Using the military strength of their Mongol allies for leverage, the Gelugpa sect quickly gained political might. By 1642, when the fifth Dalai Lama en-

> *I revolted against the Lama order because I was so often flogged.*
>
> —TZUMEN JENDZE
> a Tibetan who, as a child,
> was given by his parents to
> a monastery in Lhasa

listed the Mongols' support to overthrow the king of Tsang (the area around Lhasa), the Gelugpa became the rulers of Tibet.

But in later years the various Dalai Lamas often became more significant as mere pawns in power struggles than as spiritual figures. Political intrigues claimed the lives of more than one Dalai Lama and many other important Gelugpa figures over the next several generations. This too was part of the tradition that the young 14th Dalai Lama had entered.

Tenzin Gyatso would learn the harsh lessons of politics soon enough, but in the meantime he was kept busy with the more formal aspects of the Gelugpa tradition. The monastic education was rigorous for any monk, but for Tenzin Gyatso, who as Dalai Lama was expected to embody all the greatest virtues of the Gelugpa order, it was exceedingly demanding. First he had to learn how to read and write. This alone was unusual; most novice lamas did not learn these skills, which were considered worldly and thus a hindrance to spiritual development. But beyond merely learning the language,

Tibetan nuns in the early 1900s. There were 15,000 women in Tibet's nunneries during Tenzin Gyatso's reign, about one-tenth the number of monks. Women held high status in family life and many had more than one husband (when marrying a man it was possible to marry his younger brothers at the same time), but they held low status in religious life.

Tenzin Gyatso was expected to learn all four distinct forms of the Tibetan script. While he was grappling with the intricacies of reading, writing, grammar, and spelling in the four forms of the language, Tenzin Gyatso was also introduced to the "five minor subjects": drama, dance and music, astrology, poetry, and composition.

Tenzin Gyatso had a number of teachers, all of them renowned authorities in the Gelugpa tradition, but two of them would remain his closest guides and advisers for the rest of their lives. One of Tenzin Gyatso's tutors, Trijiang Rinpoche, who taught him the rudiments of spelling and grammar, was well known throughout Tibet's monastic world for his lectures on Buddhism. The most brilliant scholar, however, was the junior tutor, Ling Rinpoche. (*Rinpoche* is an honorific title given to leading lamas; it means "precious.") Whenever Ling Rinpoche was teaching, he hung a silk whip on the wall and would stare at it meaningfully if Tenzin Gyatso's interest waned. But the tactic was purely for effect; the whip was never used.

In 1944, after spending five years perfecting his command of written Tibetan, it was time for the young Dalai Lama to begin his study of "the higher subjects," which included medicine, Sanskrit, logic, fine arts, metaphysics, and the philosophy of religion. The last of these was considered the most important in the Tibetan system, particularly in the Dalai Lama's education. At the age of 12, Tenzin Gyatso had to memorize long essays on these higher subjects and take part in discussions with some of Tibet's most learned scholars. "At first it was not very easy," the Dalai Lama later admitted, "but soon the difficulties disappeared and the subjects became most agreeable."

The young student specialized in a long philosophical text known as the Prajnaparamita, or "The Perfection of Wisdom." As he would soon be examined on his knowledge of this text, Tenzin Gyatso had to memorize not only the fundamental principles of the treatise itself but also 2 long commentaries, one of which consisted of 302 pages written by the fifth Dalai Lama. Each day he would learn

The Potala was an enormous storehouse. Here were rooms full of thousands of priceless scrolls. There were strong rooms filled with the golden regalia of the earliest kings of Tibet.

—TENZIN GYATSO
THE DALAI LAMA

about a third of a page by heart and read a great deal more. At the same time he began his training in elementary logic and debate. At this point he was being instructed by seven monks from the seven largest monasteries of Tibet.

Apart from the regular curriculum of Tibetan education, Tenzin Gyatso found a welcome diversion in the company of an Austrian fugitive from a British prisoner-of-war camp in India. The Austrian, whose name was Heinrich Harrer, arrived in Lhasa in 1946 after an epic 20-month journey across Tibet. When Tenzin Gyatso heard of Harrer's arrival he had the foreigner summoned to the Potala, and plied him with innumerable questions about the outside world. Harrer soon became a familiar face around the Potala and something of a tutor to the Dalai Lama, to whom he taught English, geography, and mathematics. Harrer also helped to shape the young ruler's perception of the complex world of international politics. Together, they would watch British newsreel films in the projection room of the Potala and discuss the new order that was emerging in the world with the defeat of the German and Japanese forces in World War II.

The months passed swiftly. Soon after Tenzin Gyatso turned 13 in August 1948, he was called to undergo public tests toward his admission to the 2 prestigious monasteries of Drepung and Sera. It must have seemed a daunting task for a teenager, even one who had spent the better part of his life in study.

The youthful Dalai Lama was expected to take part in public debates on Buddhist scriptures. His opponents in these discussions were the abbots of the monasteries, perhaps the most experienced men alive in the intricacies of Gelugpa debates. The debates were not merely a matter of men speaking to each other and trading points and counterpoints. They were a highly ritualized art form that involved movement, dance, and the ability to recite verbatim long passages from any one of scores of sacred texts. When a speaker raised a certain point or quoted from a certain text, he had to accompany his assertion with the appropriate body posture, while at

He seemed to me like a person who had for years brooded in solitude over different problems, and now that he had at least someone to talk to wanted to know all the answers at once.
—HEINRICH HARRER
Austrian writer, on the
14-year-old Dalai Lama

the same time the listener had to hold his body a certain way. Also, the debates were performed before a large audience, composed of the massed congregation of the monasteries — hundreds of religious dignitaries and thousands of regular monks. Tenzin Gyatso understandably felt, as he later put it, "a little worried" as the debates approached. But his performance was impressive, and his learned examiners were left more than satisfied.

The debates at Drepung and Sera were not the last nor the most severe tests that Tenzin Gyatso would have to face in the course of his academic training. Buddhism, according to the Dalai Lama, is "an intellectual rather than an emotional religion, and it has a literature of thousands of volumes, of which I studied hundreds." All the same it would be a mistake to assume that Tenzin Gyatso's youth was consumed in the enforced drudgery of reading and memorizing religious texts; on the contrary, he seems to have revelled in his tasks. He later wrote that "my interest reached beyond my allotted studies, and I found satisfaction in reading advanced chapters of the books and wanting to know from my teachers more than I was supposed to at my age."

But whatever pleasure he may have derived from it, all this solitary study must have left Tenzin Gyatso a somewhat lonely boy. He had no classmates and knew little of life in the city that sprawled below the Potala palace. His family life was not of a common nature either. Although a house had been built for his parents halfway between the Potala and the city below, the pressures of his training allowed him to visit them only once every six weeks.

Nevertheless, even though he was to some extent imprisoned in his palace, the child in the young incarnate lama found escapes and diversions. He explored the cavernous expanses of the palace, which was practically a city in itself. Often he would spend hours in a musty and cold room in the north wall of the Potala, from which he could watch the busy streets of Lhasa. As evening fell he would hear the sounds of young children singing as they walked their cattle home from pasture, and he would often wonder what it would be like to live their lives.

There between my lessons, I could walk and run among the flowers and orchards and the peacocks and the tame musk deer.

—TENZIN GYATSO
THE DALAI LAMA
on the Norbulingka, his
summer palace

A lama of Sera monastery during a theological debate. The young Dalai Lama excelled in the highly ritualized debates, during which a debater must assume certain body postures when raising or rebutting points on Buddhist theology.

For all his loneliness, the approach of summer brought a welcome change of scene to Tenzin Gyatso, who would move from the Potala to the Norbulingka palace on the outskirts of Lhasa for the season. Here he enjoyed a less formal atmosphere than what he was accustomed to in the Potala, and found time to relish the parks and lakes of the palace gardens.

If the young Dalai Lama had any pleasures to rival the attention he gave to his religious studies, it must have been his interest in mechanical objects. Throughout his childhood he was provided with a wide variety of mechanical toys and other equipment, ranging from electrical generators to movie projectors, all of which he proceeded to take apart and occasionally reassemble. In time he graduated to tinkering with some broken-down cars he found on the grounds of the Norbulingka, and he soon had them in working order.

It was an idyllic time for Tenzin Gyatso, but it would not last for long. Soon the harsh realities of politics would transform his peaceful world into one of crisis and bloodshed.

4

The Big Family of the Motherland

Despite the deeply religious nature of the Gelugpa order, its leading members were not above resorting to violence in political matters — a tendency that made the order no different from religious institutions or organizations that held governmental power in other nations.

Indeed, Lhasa had seen more than its share of political intrigues in the years between the 13th Dalai Lama's death in 1933 and Tenzin Gyatso's installation in the Potala in 1940. Just three days after the death of the Great 13th, for example, the finance minister led a regiment of troops in an attempt to seize control of the Tibetan government. The rest of the Kshag ministers ultimately regained control and punished the rebellious minister by having him blinded. The next intrigue would involve Tenzin Gyatso more closely.

Here [Tibet], as all over China, accelerated metamorphosis was going on; I would see the time machine gather speed, and space, that great beast, laid low by human toil. And this was a miracle greater than all reputed divine agencies could muster.
—HAN SUYIN
Chinese author

Tenzin Gyatso receives an urn containing the ashes of two of the Buddha's disciples in the southern Tibetan monastery of Dungkar in 1951, after he had fled Lhasa to escape the invading Chinese army. China invaded Tibet in October 1950, and by 1952 its occupation of Tibet was complete.

The high lama Reting Rinpoche (seated), who acted as regent and ruled Tibet in young Tenzin Gyatso's name from 1937 until 1941, when he heeded the advice of an oracle and retired. In 1947 he tried to return to the post, sparking a brief civil war, which he lost. A week after he was captured and imprisoned, he was found dead in a Potala dungeon.

In 1941, one year after Tenzin Gyatso had been installed in the Potala, his regent Reting Rinpoche went to the monastery that housed the Oracle of Nechung, a lama credited with the ability to foretell the future. The oracle told Reting Rinpoche that he should withdraw from his post as regent if he wanted to live much longer. The regent, knowing that he was unpopular with many powerful Tibetans who resented his close ties with the Chinese government, heeded the oracle's advice.

Accordingly, Reting Rinpoche retired altogether from the demands of his political role in order to resume his monastic duties for a time. The regency was then given to Taktra Rinpoche, another incarnate lama and also the Dalai Lama's senior tutor. Taktra Rinpoche was given the post with the understanding that Reting Rinpoche would one day return to the position.

By 1947, six years had passed since Reting Rinpoche had handed the regency over to Taktra Rinpoche. During that time Taktra Rinpoche's government had acquired a reputation for corruption and inefficiency, and Reting Rinpoche apparently felt it was time to return from his religious retreat in the monastery of Sera to take control of the regency himself.

Considerable tension arose between the supporters of the two lamas. Finally, Reting Rinpoche's followers attempted, unsuccessfully, to assassinate Taktra Rinpoche, and in consequence Reting Rinpoche was arrested. The arrest sparked a violent revolt by his supporters in the monastery of Sera, and for two weeks a battle raged between monks and government troops. Hundreds were killed before the monks surrendered. A week later Reting Rinpoche was found dead in his cell in the dungeons of the Potala.

This brief but sordid incident had revealed the weak and divided nature of Tibet's government during the regency. To many Tibetans the bloody clash between the two lamas was clear evidence that the 13th Dalai Lama's prophecies of doom for the nation would be fulfiled. All that remained to completely fulfil the Great 13th's prophecy was for a foreign power to take advantage of Tibet's weakness.

It was not hard to guess where the greatest threat lay. China was by now in the final phase of the long revolution that would bring the Communist party and its leader, Mao Zedong, to power. China, the world's most populous country and Tibet's neighbour to the east, would be ruled under strict communist precepts: Private ownership of goods and property was largely outlawed and religion was virtually banned. Furthermore, the success of the revolution would leave China newly united, strengthened, and anxious for territorial expansion.

China had a long history of involvement in Tibetan affairs. In 1720, during a Tibetan civil war between a Chinese-backed king of Amdo and a Mongol-backed regent, the emperor of China sent in an army that took Lhasa and installed the seventh Dalai Lama. China annexed most of Kham and all of Amdo provinces and established an overlordship in Tibet that would last almost 200 years. The Chinese emperor allowed the Dalai Lama to rule Tibet in all matters of religion and local government but retained control of the country's foreign affairs by stationing two Chinese governors and a small garrison of troops in Lhasa. A bloody revolt against the Chinese governors in Lhasa in 1750 was the only major Tibetan rebellion against Chinese rule.

The forces of Mao Zedong (pictured here around 1950), chairman of the Chinese Communist party and leader of China, won a long civil war in 1949 and united China under one ruler for the first time in three decades. Under Mao, China immediately sought to regain all the territory it had lost since the 19th century — including Tibet.

The Chinese also had an important ally among the Tibetans themselves: the Panchen Lama, an incarnate lama roughly equal in status to the Dalai Lama. The institution of the Panchen Lama was initiated by the fifth Dalai Lama, who in gratitude to his tutor declared him a reincarnation of Erpame, the Bodhisattva of the Boundless Light, and made him chief lama of the huge Trashilhunpo monastery. Tibetan Buddhists considered Erpame a greater bodhisattva than Chenrezi, but the Dalai Lama was nevertheless regarded as slightly more important than the Panchen Lama. By the 1800s, the Dalai Lama was esteemed as Tibet's highest authority in spiritual matters, and the Panchen Lama (which means "Learned Lama") was usually considered supreme in political affairs. Disputes between the two highest lamas inevitably occurred, and the Chinese governors tended to side with the Panchen Lama to keep the Dalai Lama from becoming powerful enough to challenge Chinese rule.

During the 13th Dalai Lama's reign, which began in 1876, the Chinese overlordship in Tibet slowly disintegrated under the pressure of Great Britain,

The 11-year-old Panchen Lama (seated) in a Tsinghai monastery in 1948. Born and raised in China and just two years younger than the Dalai Lama, whom he rivalled as Tibet's spiritual leader, Buddhists believed him to be the 10th reincarnation of the first Panchen Lama. Disputes between the various Dalai and Panchen Lamas had plagued Tibet since the early 1800s.

which by then controlled India, Nepal, Sikkim, Bhutan, and Burma. In 1904, seeking to expand the British empire north of the Himalayas, a British force invaded Tibet and, after six months of fighting in which several thousand Tibetans were killed, entered Lhasa. The 13th Dalai Lama fled to Mongolia, but his regent, the ninth Panchen Lama, remained behind to rule Tibet and signed a truce with the British.

The 13th Dalai Lama remained in Mongolia for three years and in Beijing, China's capital, for one year before returning to Lhasa in December 1909. But within a month he was forced to flee once again, this time because a Chinese army, summoned by the Panchen Lama, was marching toward the capital to reestablish Chinese rule. The Chinese lasted one year in Tibet. They withdrew in 1911 when the emperor of China was overthrown by Chinese nationalists who set up a representative government in Beijing.

In 1912, the 13th Dalai Lama returned to Lhasa from his exile in India. He stripped the Panchen Lama of many of his privileges and declared Tibet's independence; Tibet, he asserted, had belonged to the Chinese emperor, and now that the emperor had been overthrown, Tibet was free. The Chinese nationalist government rejected his claim, but lacked the military power to retake Tibet. Soon most of China fell under the control of local warlords, and in 1924, the Chinese-supported Panchen Lama fled to China. Tibet was left alone, secure within its mountain borders.

In the 1930s, Japan invaded and brutally occupied eastern China; its armies were finally driven out in 1945. A second Chinese revolution then broke out, and in 1949, the Chinese Communists under Mao routed the nationalists from mainland China. A strong central government was in place in Beijing for the first time in the 20th century, and it quickly turned its attentions to Tibet.

On New Year's Day, 1950, Radio Beijing, the voice of the newly established People's Republic of China, announced the future objectives of the victorious People's Liberation Army (PLA). Tibet, the announc-

A road is not only a highway for rolling vehicles; it is an instrument for change, and very early the great prelates, the pontiffs and the lords, seeing it built, must have felt time was not on their side. The wheel was here, and it meant that a great many things, including the fact that trade (which had been in the hands of noble families and merchant-lamas) would now also be altered.
—HAN SUYIN
Chinese author

A block of houses in Lhasa are dwarfed by the Potala, where on January 1, 1950, the Dalai Lama's advisers heard the Radio Beijing broadcast announcing China's intent to "liberate" Tibet. The Tibetan government immediately mobilized its poorly equipped 10,000-man army in preparation for a Chinese invasion.

er declared, "had fallen under the influence of foreign imperialists" and would have to be "liberated" in order to "secure China's western borders." The broadcast was heard by the monks in the Potala. They knew instantly that Tibet's nearly 40 years of peaceful isolation from the outside world was about to end.

The government in Lhasa began a belated and lumbering attempt to react to the unmistakable threat in the Chinese broadcast. Its first concern was quite naturally for the army. Tibet's armed forces were not very formidable; with only some 10,000 troops, the poorly trained army also lacked equipment and ammunition. Although fresh troops were quickly enlisted to strengthen the border garrisons, there was little hope that they could defeat a determined offensive by the battle-hardened PLA, which had spent the previous decade fighting the Japanese and the forces of the Chinese nationalists.

Accordingly, the Lhasa government began efforts to win diplomatic guarantees from other nations — Britain, the United States, and newly independent India — that they would not tolerate a Chinese invasion of Tibet. But these efforts proved futile. Tibet had no formal diplomatic relations with any nation other than India, and even India had mixed feelings about Tibet's status as an independent nation. Finally, with no prospect of foreign support in sight, the Tibetans decided to negotiate with Beijing.

The Chinese, however, had little interest in negotiations. In June 1950, a small PLA force — already in southwestern China for operations against the few remaining anticommunist warlords in the area — crossed the border and launched the offensive against Tibet by seizing the Tibetan border town of Dengkog. Two weeks later the Tibetans recaptured it, but these relatively minor engagements only served as a prelude to the main event. In October of the same year the Chinese attacked in earnest, crossing the Yangtze river into Tibet with an army of 84,000 troops. The PLA seized several towns before the Tibetan generals could make a move to stop them. In a matter of days, the Chinese held most of the strategic mountain passes that led into Kham, Tibet's easternmost province.

The first prize to fall into Chinese hands was Kham's provincial capital, Chamdo. There, the recently appointed governor of Kham, an aristocrat named Ngawang Ngabo, had panicked and ordered the Tibetan garrison to surrender to a small advance guard of Chinese troops. The local population — the Khampas, known for their fierce and warlike ways — were so demoralized by the surrender that they offered little resistance themselves; in fact, many chose to work as guides for the Chinese. By October 25, 1950, just 12 days after the offensive had got under way, the PLA was in firm control of Kham.

China's leaders were confident that the rest of the kingdom could be taken without further bloodshed. After all, the Tibetan forces were completely demoralized, and the PLA had captured both Ngawang Ngabo and the Dalai Lama's oldest brother, Taktser Rinpoche, a lama and government administrator. The Chinese hoped to use these important Tibetan officials as bargaining chips in negotiating the surrender of Lhasa. Ngawang Ngabo added to the pressure by sending messages advising the Lhasa government to surrender; this was the beginning of his long career as a collabourator with the Chinese occupation forces.

Meanwhile in Lhasa, panic was spreading among the populace and the lamas of the Potala. The government sought advice from the Oracle of Nechung,

A Tibetan soldier stands at attention in the 1930s. The army of Tibet, a protectorate of China from 1720 to 1911, was used mostly in internal power struggles. In 1904 Tibet's army was crushed by an invading British force, and during Tibet's post-1911 period of independence it saw little action. In 1950 it would prove no match for China's People's Liberation Army (PLA).

A PLA truck convoy moves out of Chamdo, the capital of Kham province in eastern Tibet, in late 1950. The PLA invasion force of 84,000 troops, which crossed into Tibet in October 1950, needed just 12 days to overcome the Tibetan army and take Kham.

the lama who had once advised Reting Rinpoche to give up the regency. The oracle had only one command: that Tenzin Gyatso should be crowned and take control of the government himself. And indeed this did seem to be the only reasonable option remaining. Although the Dalai Lama was just 15 years old, he was the only figure around whom any organized patriotic resistance to the Chinese could gather.

Tenzin Gyatso himself was filled with anxiety when his advisers requested him to assume the throne. He protested that at 15, he was still 3 years away from the accepted age at which a Dalai Lama could legally take over governmental duties. But when the Tsongdu met and added its voice to the advisers' request, he realized that it was time to "put his boyhood behind him," as he later put it. Full powers were conferred upon him in a traditional ceremony followed by celebrations and a general amnesty, in which every convict in Tibet was given his freedom.

For all the festivities surrounding Tenzin Gyatso's investiture, there was little cause for happiness. Only days after the ceremonies were concluded, Tibet's new ruler received more dire news from his brother Taktser Rinpoche, who had been released by the Chinese after falsely promising to assist them in toppling the Tibetan government. His reports left little doubt of China's intention to expand its control over the rest of Tibet.

Fears soon arose for the safety of the Dalai Lama. It was finally decided that Tenzin Gyatso should leave the capital for the southern border town of Yatung, from where it would be easy to escape to India. Despite the Dalai Lama's own unhappiness about leaving Lhasa to the advancing Chinese army, arrangements were swiftly made to flee the city. For the first time since his arrival in Lhasa 11 years earlier, Tenzin Gyatso found himself outside the region of the capital.

It must have been an eventful journey for the young ruler. As the royal caravan proceeded out of Lhasa, it found its path blocked by hundreds of distraught monks who begged their leader not to abandon them. Having spent years of seclusion in the Potala, Tenzin Gyatso was not accustomed to such public appeals. But rising to the occasion he spoke directly to the lamas, assuring them that he would return.

Once the party arrived in Yatung, the teenage Dalai Lama realized that the many years he spent poring over the scriptures had readied him for his religious and ceremonial duties, but had given him little preparation for his new role as the leader of a country at war. Most previous Dalai Lamas had stayed aloof from political and military matters, leaving the kingdom in the hands of others while they withdrew into a life of prayer and study. Other

The Oracle of Nechung, whom Tibetans believe has the ability to see the future. As panic spread in Lhasa over the threat of a PLA attack against the city, the oracle commanded that the 15-year-old Dalai Lama ascend the throne and lead the Tibetan government. Accordingly, Tenzin Gyatso was crowned on November 17, 1950.

Dalai Lamas, like the 13th, had been vigourous political leaders, playing a decisive and sometimes brutal role in the defence of their kingdom. Only time would tell what kind of a leader Tenzin Gyatso would be.

A Tibetan delegation had already been sent to negotiate with the Chinese government, but upon their arrival in Beijing the delegation was forced under threat of violence to accept terms of complete surrender. One evening in May 1951, as the Dalai Lama and his closest advisers gathered around a shortwave radio in Yatung, they were shocked to hear the voice of Ngawang Ngabo delivering a speech stating to the world the terms of the Chinese takeover of Tibet. "The Tibetan people shall return to the big family of the motherland," he announced, "the People's Republic of China." Tibet had ceased to be an independent nation. It would retain control of all religious and internal affairs, but all military matters and foreign relations would be controlled by China. In effect, the old Chinese overlordship that had lasted from 1720 until the beginning of the 20th century was being restored.

A few days later the Dalai Lama received a telegram informing him that a Chinese general was coming to meet him in Yatung. This news prompted some to urge the Dalai Lama to flee to India, as many important families from Lhasa had already done. Tenzin Gyatso himself had even persuaded his old friend and companion Heinrich Harrer to leave for India. But the many who had stayed, particularly the high incarnate lamas, encouraged Tenzin Gyatso to remain in Tibet to help his people deal with the Chinese occupation. He agreed, and stayed in Yatung to await the arrival of the Chinese general.

The general, Zhang Jingwu, arrived one morning in July for the negotiations, which turned out to be fairly informal and relaxed. Zhang reassured the Dalai Lama that Tibet would continue to have a high degree of independence as a self-governing province within the Chinese nation; at the same time he urged the Dalai Lama to return to Lhasa. The young ruler had no choice but to agree. On August 17, 1951, he returned to the capital.

There are three great lacks in Tibet: fuel, communication, and people. And there were three great abundances before. Poverty, oppression, and the terror of the supernatural. The three latter caused the former.
—COMRADE ZHEN
Chinese woman living in Tibet, interviewed by Chinese author Han Suyin

Meanwhile, PLA forces had entrenched themselves in Kham and sent large detachments toward Lhasa. In September, the first detachment of some 3,000 Chinese troops arrived at the outskirts of the capital, and a month later they were reinforced by an additional 5,000 soldiers. Although the Chinese forces were disciplined and restrained in their treatment of the civilian population, they had arrived in the city with few supplies of their own and requisitioned food from the Tibetans in large quantities. By 1952, there was a serious food shortage in the capital, deepening the Lhasans' resentment of the foreign troops in their city. Chinese soldiers were spat upon and stoned in the streets. Posters denouncing the invaders appeared on walls all over Lhasa.

In the midst of all this hostility, the young Dalai Lama was thrust into a particularly uncomfortable position. On the one hand, he remained a living symbol of independent Tibet. On the other hand, his continued presence in Lhasa depended on his maintaining good relations with the PLA commanders in the city. As tension between the Lhasans and the PLA mounted, Tenzin Gyatso realized he would have to tread a fine line in the days to come.

Ngawang Ngabo (left), the governor of Kham, and Mao Zedong at a state dinner in Beijing in 1951. Ngawang Ngabo collaborated with the Chinese invaders and in May 1951 announced that China would rule Tibet. The Dalai Lama, who had fled Lhasa six months earlier, learned of the announcement in the southern Tibetan town of Yatung.

5

The Dictates of the Overlords

When Tenzin Gyatso returned to the Potala in 1951 he was unsure of what role he would play in Chinese-ruled Tibet. He had no real experience in power politics, but he knew that most Tibetans would look to him for leadership. It remained unclear how much authority the Chinese would be willing to allow him, but for the moment it seemed that the PLA commanders needed him to administer the new Chinese province of Tibet.

Although he was only 16 years old, the Dalai Lama was well aware of the complexities of his position. He knew that the Chinese were anxious to exploit the loyal support he had from the majority of Tibetans. At the same time he was aware that Tibetans would be watching to see whether he was collaborating too closely with the Chinese. For their part, the PLA generals who represented the Chinese government in Tibet followed a policy of maintaining outwardly friendly and respectful relations with the Dalai Lama while simultaneously going to great lengths to restrict his political and spiritual authority.

If you hit a man on the head and break his skull, you can hardly expect him to be friendly.
—LUKHANGWA
the Dalai Lama's minister, in response to complaints about anti-Chinese behaviour

The Panchen Lama (left), Mao Zedong (centre), and the Dalai Lama in Beijing in 1956. Five years earlier the Dalai Lama had accepted Chinese rule and returned to Lhasa to preside over the government, but he soon found that he was little more than a figurehead who was being used to legitimize the Chinese occupation.

The Chinese abolished many of the elaborate rituals that were the traditional symbols of the Dalai Lama's status as the incarnation of Chenrezi and as the king of Tibet. For example, it had long been considered a rare privilege for ordinary Tibetans to look upon the Dalai Lama, and anyone doing so was required to kneel before him. The Chinese, however, tried to give such encounters a more ordinary character; two years after the PLA's arrival in Lhasa they announced that the Dalai Lama would meet any Tibetan wishing to petition him with a request. The reform turned out to be a refreshing change for the teenage god-king, who felt he had been sheltered in the reverential company of the Potala's high lamas for long enough. Moreover, he shared the Chinese belief that Tibet's political system was hopelessly outdated and welcomed the opportunity to learn more about the common people.

During his childhood Tenzin Gyatso had had little contact with ordinary Tibetans, seeing them only on ceremonial occasions — and then, only from behind a gauze screen so that he could watch without being seen. But these ceremonies in Lhasa had little to do with the lives of the Tibetan peasants scattered in isolated villages throughout the vast kingdom. Tenzin Gyatso realized, as he later put it, that "most people in the distant marches of Tibet had never been to Lhasa, or even perhaps met anyone who had been there. From year to year, they tilled the earth and bred their yaks and other animals and neither heard nor saw what happened in the world beyond their own horizon."

Apart from the settled peasantry, Tibet also had a large population of nomads, who roamed the vast and empty plains with their herds of yaks and sheep. Although they lived a generally peaceful existence in their camps of black-felt tents, the nomads were feared by traders whose caravans they sometimes plundered. Indeed there were few sights that would strike more fear into the heart of a settled Tibetan than a band of galloping nomads, their heavy silver amulets clattering a warning as they rode, their broad swords flashing in the sun. But apart from the occasional brigandage of the no-

mads, there was little overt social conflict in Tibetan society. Although most rural Tibetans were poor, they generally were able to provide for their needs.

Nevertheless, Tibet had a very inequitable social structure, in which the monasteries and a few aristocratic families owned most of the nation's land and wealth, while the majority of Tibetans lived in relative poverty as peasants and labourers. Most monasteries and aristocratic clans extracted taxes and labour from the peasantry in order to sustain their own opulent way of life. During his journey to Yatung, the Dalai Lama had had his first opportunity to see the conditions in which many of his subjects lived; now, at the prodding of the Chinese Communist occupiers, he resolved to do something to improve those conditions.

A Tibetan nomad family in the icy, sparsely populated mountains of Changthang province. Nomads there and in Kham province sometimes engaged in banditry, and one of the Chinese government's stated reasons for invading Tibet was to put an end to it, both in Tibet and in south-western China.

The women of a powerful aristocratic family in Lhasa. Until the arrival of the Chinese, hereditary nobles and high lamas controlled Tibet's government and wealth.

In late 1951, the Dalai Lama set up a reforms committee, called the Lekche, to study and report to him on possible measures to improve the economic condition of the poor. In response to the Lekche's report he introduced a number of significant reforms. Taxes on peasants were reduced and farmers who had difficulty repaying loans were given financial relief in various forms, sometimes being relieved of their debts altogether. Laws were passed to prevent landlords from making excessive demands on their peasant tenants, and state-owned lands were divided up and given to the landless labourers who had been working on them.

But Tenzin Gyatso's reforms did little to change the centuries-old system of land ownership, and they were far too mild to satisfy the Chinese authorities. They quickly stepped in to introduce more wide-reaching reforms that were more in keeping with their communist convictions. The Chinese military government seized the land owned by many of Tibet's powerful nobles and redistributed it to the peasant families who had toiled there for generations. The Chinese also took many other measures that were undeniably helpful to the mass of Tibet's poor cultivators, providing them with cash and seed grains with which to improve their crop, building the nation's first reliable roads, and instituting a system of medical services that included the construction of several new hospitals and the use of mobile medical units to bring doctors to remote villages.

The Chinese efforts to improve the quality of life of the Tibetan peasants certainly reflected their belief that they were bringing social and political progress to the Land of Snows. From a more pragmatic standpoint, however, the Chinese government had much more to gain by their control of Tibet. The PLA was now deployed in a strong strategic position in the Himalayas, face to face with India, the other major power in Asia in the 1950s. Moreover, Tibet offered vast unexploited resources of land and mineral deposits, both of which were important to the Chinese government's goal of greatly improving agricultural and industrial development throughout China.

Peasants threshing grain in southeastern Tibet. Most of the nation's land was owned by the monasteries, nobles, and the Dalai Lama himself and was worked by or leased to peasants. When the Chinese took over Tibet they introduced communist land reforms, breaking up the large estates and redistributing the land to the peasants.

Thus the Chinese regarded Tibet as an important strategic asset. Control of the province and of the potentially rebellious population was vital. At first the Chinese allowed the Dalai Lama to keep his leading government advisers, but after the aides became too vocal in their criticism of the PLA the Chinese forced him to dismiss them. Nevertheless, the Beijing government still courted Tenzin Gyatso's support.

In 1954, the Dalai Lama received an invitation to visit the Chinese leaders in Beijing, and he accepted. Thousands of anxious Lhasans turned out to bid him farewell as he was setting out on the trip to the Chinese capital in July of that year; many of them were fearful that he would not be allowed to return.

Accompanied by an entourage of high government and religious figures — which included his tutors Ling Rinpoche and Trijiang Rinpoche, his mother, two of his brothers, and his older sister Tsering Dolma with her husband, P. T. Takala, the head of the royal guard — the Dalai Lama headed for Beijing in a convoy along the newly built Chinese highway from Lhasa to the city of Chengtu in the Chinese province of Sichuan. They proceeded slowly, losing several mules and one car to the sheer precipices and surging rivers they had to cross en route to Sichuan. Once in Chengtu, the Tibetans were flown to the city of Xian, where they boarded a special train to Beijing; both the aeroplane flight and the train ride were firsts for the Dalai Lama. "Only a few years before, when mechanical things so interested me," Tenzin Gyatso would later say of his journey, "flying or travelling by train would have seemed like a glorious dream. But now that I was doing them both for the first time, my mind was much too full of our political misfortunes for me to enjoy these new experiences."

The Dalai Lama was joined on the final leg of his journey by the 16-year-old 10th Panchen Lama. Like Tenzin Gyatso, he too had been born in Tsinghai. But the Panchen Lama had spent his boyhood in China, first in the hands of the nationalist Chinese, then in the hands of the communist Chinese, and

I was greatly impressed by Mao Zedong's outstanding personality. . . . His appearance gave no sign of his intellectual power. . . . Yet his manner of speech captured the minds and imaginations of his listeners, and gave the impression of kindness and sincerity. . . . I was convinced that he himself would never use force to convert Tibet into a communist state.
—TENZIN GYATSO
THE DALAI LAMA
on his visit to China

was now being used by the Beijing regime to justify their rule of Tibet. He was finally installed in Tibet by the Chinese conquerors in 1952 — the first time since 1924 that a Panchen Lama had resided in Tibet — and as a result the young lama commonly made statements supporting Chinese policies in Tibet. But the Dalai Lama sensed that "left to himself he would have whole-heartedly supported Tibet against the inroads of China."

Upon his arrival in Beijing, the Dalai Lama was greeted with much fanfare. Several banquets were held in his honour, attended by the leading figures of the Chinese Communist party. When he finally met Mao Zedong, the chairman of the party and the Chinese head of state, Tenzin Gyatso found him to be "a simple man of dignity and authority." His discussions with Mao on the situation in Tibet, he later reported, were relatively frank, and he appealed to the chairman to rein in the PLA occupying forces. Mao promised that the military administration in the area would soon be replaced by a civilian body, to be called the Preparatory Committee for the Autonomous Region of Tibet.

Tenzin Gyatso lectures at a Buddhist temple in Beijing in 1954. The young Dalai Lama met Mao Zedong during his six-month stay in the Chinese capital and found Mao "a simple man of dignity and authority."

The Dalai Lama and his party spent six months in Beijing. In that time the Tibetan delegation was impressed by what they saw of the advances the Chinese government had made in developing their nation's agriculture and industry — advances they promised to bring to Tibet. Although the Dalai Lama had been apprehensive about the manner in which the Chinese went about the modernization of Tibet, he now felt reassured that the province would be governed more gently and allowed to maintain its autonomy.

If Tenzin Gyatso came away from Beijing with some optimism for the future, he had not lost sight of the political realities that faced him. He knew that he would still have to walk a tightrope between the

The Chinese flag flies overhead as the Dalai Lama and the Panchen Lama flank Chinese vice-premier Chen Yi (saluting, second from right) during a 1956 ceremony in Lhasa marking the formation of a committee to reorganize Tibet as a province of China. The Dalai Lama was named chairman of the committee and the Panchen Lama its vice-chairman.

defence of his country's interests and the need to maintain good relations with the Chinese, but he felt he could face the challenge. His older brother Lobsang Samten said of him: "When he went to Beijing he was no more than a boy. He learned many things there and when he came back he could make decisions for himself."

As things turned out, the Dalai Lama's optimism was ill founded, and he would need his newly acquired political skills more than ever. While he had been away, the resentment of many citizens in Kham — the region that had been under Chinese rule the longest — had boiled over. Ironically, the Chinese had received a relatively friendly welcome in Kham when they had first marched in, and many

Khampas had joined the Chinese forces and served as guides for the PLA during the invasion of the rest of Tibet. But the Khampas soon grew hostile to the Chinese. As in the rest of Tibet, thousands of Khampas were forced to serve as road-construction labourers, and many had died during the dangerous work of building roads through the treacherous mountain passes. Khampa landowners, affronted by the new land reforms, also chafed under Chinese rule and led an insurrection against the PLA in the province in 1955. The Chinese military retaliated by bombing a large monastery, killing most of the monks who lived there. The Khampas reacted by stepping up the insurrection into a full-scale armed rebellion. News of these developments was kept from the Dalai Lama until the spring of 1956.

In April 1956, the Preparatory Committee, the body that would ease Tibet's transition from military to civilian rule, was inaugurated in Lhasa. Although the Dalai Lama was made chairman of the committee, it did not take him long to see that he was once again being used to lend authority to an institution with which he had no common purpose. The committee had been filled with pro-Chinese members, and in any case it was not permitted to pass any resolutions that were not approved by the Committee of the Chinese Communist Party in Tibet—a body that had no Tibetan members.

Meanwhile, in Lhasa itself, anti-Chinese feelings were mounting daily. During the Buddhist new year's festival of Monlam, in early 1956, posters and pamphlets appeared all over the city calling on Tibetans to "shed our blood and sacrifice our lives to oppose the Communists." The period of Monlam celebrations was traditionally a time when rural Tibetans converged on Lhasa, both to assert their faith and to sample the pleasures of city life. Under Chinese occupation the festival had become a time to rally support for the old order and challenge the new. During the Monlam of 1954, the Chinese authorities had tried to restrict religious activities but had met with violence when soldier-monks known as Dob-dobs had hacked a group of PLA soldiers to death for challenging the Dob-dobs' traditional

By its geographical location, Tibet is of extreme strategic importance; it is the very heart of Asia, the advance post of China's south-west, a bastion of colossal size, dominating the hinterland. Its defence is of decisive importance to China.
—HAN SUYIN
Chinese author

A Tibetan exile bows to the Dalai Lama during his six-month trip to India in 1956–57 for celebrations marking the 2,500th anniversary of the birth of the Buddha. Many family members and Tibetan officials urged the Dalai Lama to stay in India but he refused, preferring to use his influence to temper the Chinese occupation of Tibet.

right to police Lhasa during the festival. On that occasion the Chinese authorities had retreated, but by 1956 they were no longer in a conciliatory mood. The PLA commanders forced the Dalai Lama to agree to the arrest of the leaders of the anti-Chinese movement in Lhasa.

This was the latest in a string of events in which Tenzin Gyatso had consented to Chinese actions against his people, and it weighed heavily on his conscience. He knew that most Tibetans remained passionately loyal to him but admitted, "I do not flatter myself that I earned this loyalty by personal qualities of my own. It was the concept of the Dalai Lama which held their loyalty. I was a symbol of what they were fighting for." He desperately wanted to leave his ambiguous political role behind him and to restrict himself to religious activities. Still, he realized that as long as he was in Tibet, he could not escape from politics.

Just as his spirits were reaching a low ebb, Tenzin Gyatso received an invitation to attend celebrations in India marking the 2,500th anniversary of the birth of the Buddha. The invitation was personally delivered to him by the Choegyal, the ruler of Sikkim, a tiny principality and Indian protectorate on the Indo-Tibetan border. Tenzin Gyatso's spirits rose at the prospect of abandoning his political worries and visiting the sacred sites where Buddha himself had taught, but the Chinese authorities initially refused the Dalai Lama permission to go. However, when the Indian government renewed the invitation and extended it to the Panchen Lama as well, the Chinese allowed Tenzin Gyatso to accept.

The Dalai Lama and his party began their descent from Lhasa to the Indian plains along a familiar route, the Yatung road, which had been improved by Chinese engineers. Beyond Yatung they continued on foot and horseback through the mountain pass that led to the Sikkimese border, where they were received by the Choegyal. From there they proceeded to India itself, reaching the Indian capital of New Delhi by plane in November 1956.

Once in India, the Dalai Lama found himself surrounded by many of the thousands of Tibetans who were now living there as refugees, including his own brothers, Taktser Rinpoche and Gyalo Thondup. For a time, Tenzin Gyatso himself seriously considered staying in India as an exile; the 2,500th anniversary celebrations had given him an opportunity to immerse himself in religious matters, and after his recent experiences of political life he was tempted to keep his distance from the turmoil of Lhasa. His own family and the members of the Kshag who had accompanied him encouraged him to remain in New Delhi.

For almost the first time, I had met people who were not Tibetans but felt true sympathy for Tibet.

—TENZIN GYATSO
THE DALAI LAMA
on his visit to India
in 1956

Ultimately, Tenzin Gyatso felt he could not abandon his people to their fate. During his stay in India he twice met with the Chinese prime minister, Zhou Enlai, who warned him that the unrest in Lhasa was reaching a critical level. The PLA, Zhou warned the Dalai Lama, was prepared to suppress by violent means a rebellion in Lhasa or anywhere else in Tibet.

"I was weary of politics," Tenzin Gyatso later wrote of his decision to return from India to Lhasa in April 1957. "Political talks had taken up most of my time in Delhi and cut short my pilgrimage. I had begun to detest them, and would gladly have retired from politics altogether if I had not had a duty to my people in Tibet."

Tenzin Gyatso, Indian prime minister Jawaharlal Nehru, and Chinese prime minister Zhou Enlai in the Indian capital of New Delhi in 1956. Before the Dalai Lama returned to Tibet, Zhou warned him that the PLA would not hesitate to use force to suppress an anti-Chinese rebel movement in Kham.

6

The Red Snows

The heavy snows of spring 1957 delayed the Dalai Lama's passage through the Nathu-La pass from India to Tibet. When he finally reached the top of the pass he saw that in place of the small prayer flags that traditionally fluttered in such places, the Chinese had placed enormous red flags and portraits of Chairman Mao.

By the time he reached Lhasa in April, the situation in Tibet had become critical. Tibetan rebels in Kham and across the border in Amdo had formed an organization known as Chushi Gangdruk (or "Four Rivers, Six Ranges," a reference to the geography of Kham and Amdo). The Gangdruk was composed of small, highly mobile units of fighters, many on horseback, which attacked small PLA outposts and convoys. The Chinese response had been to bomb the countryside where the rebels had support, but with little success. Frustrated, the PLA turned to mounting increasingly brutal attacks on villages and monasteries.

> *When you can stand on your own two feet, we will not stay here even if you ask us to.*
> —ZHANG JINGWU
> Chinese military commander, to the Tibetan cabinet

Lhasans listen as a PLA official explains that the Dalai Lama's government has been dissolved and replaced by direct military rule in the aftermath of the March 1959 revolt against the Chinese. The revolt and the PLA's suppression of it forced the Dalai Lama to flee Tibet; 30 years later he had still not returned.

Thousands of refugees who had fled the fighting in Kham and Amdo poured into Lhasa and the surrounding towns of central Tibet. The influx of refugees and the stories of Chinese atrocities they brought with them fuelled the already simmering resentments of the Lhasans. The Chushi Gangdruk secretly sent representatives to the Lhasa region to meet with the Mimang Tsongdu, the newly formed resistance movement of central Tibet, and in a June 1958 gathering of 5,000 armed men about 100 miles outside the capital, the 2 rebel groups formed an alliance. The Chinese authorities, alarmed at the upsurge in rebel activity, pressed the Dalai Lama to take action against the resistance groups. The Dalai Lama responded by sending a five-man delegation to the Gangdruk leaders to persuade the rebels to surrender, but the representatives joined the guerrillas instead.

In the autumn of 1958, the rebels wiped out a 300-man PLA garrison in the central Tibetan town of Tsethang. This prompted the commanders of the Chinese occupation forces to demand that the Tibetan army, which was still under the control of the Potala government, be sent into battle against the Gangdruk. When the Dalai Lama and the Kshag refused to agree to this, their relationship with the Chinese commanders began to deteriorate rapidly.

As armed rebels freely roamed the streets of Lhasa while Chinese envoys delivered increasingly dire threats to the Potala, the city prepared for the Monlam celebrations of March 1959. The somewhat surreal atmosphere in the capital was heightened by preparations for a 15-hour-long ceremonial debate at Tsuglakhang Temple in which Tenzin Gyatso would face 80 questioners, all high Gelugpa lamas, before an audience of 20,000 monks; if he did well in the debate, he would be awarded what amounted to a doctoral degree in metaphysics and bring his formal education to a successful conclusion. Meanwhile, the Chinese army, sensing that Lhasa might soon be in open revolt, dug heavy artillery into the hills surrounding the city to shell it into submission if necessary.

The rebellion finally broke out two weeks later. What finally ignited it was a strange request from the head political officer of the PLA forces, who interrupted a fully attended rehearsal of the ceremonial debate to demand that Tenzin Gyatso appear at a theatrical performance in the Chinese encampment; furthermore, the Dalai Lama was to come to the play unaccompanied by his attendants or armed bodyguard. This unusual breach of protocol soon had Lhasa buzzing with rumours of a Chinese plot to kidnap the Dalai Lama. Crowds soon swarmed around the walls of the Norbulingka, where the Tibetan leader was staying at the time. Armed citizens joined with a platoon of the royal guards, who cast off their Chinese-supplied uniforms and barricaded the road to the PLA base.

PLA trucks in the streets of Lhasa in 1958. A Buddhist prayer flag flies over the house on the right; a Chinese national flag over the building on the left. Anti-Chinese guerrillas from Kham joined up with rebels in the Lhasa area in 1958 to harass PLA garrisons in central Tibet.

Tibetan guerrillas with their horses. Revolting against communist land reforms, the influx of ethnic Chinese settlers, and the stripping of the monasteries' authority, mounted rebels in Kham and elsewhere in Tibet fought against PLA troops beginning in 1957. By 1959, the revolt had reached Lhasa itself.

The Dalai Lama tried to assure the PLA that no mob violence would occur, but he knew that conflict was inevitable. "I felt as if I were standing between two volcanoes," he later wrote, "each ready to explode at any moment." Sure enough, early on the morning of March 17, the Tibetans fired some shots at the Chinese positions, and a little later a brief salvo of Chinese shells landed in a pond within the Norbulingka grounds. The exchange was over quickly, no one was hurt, but the capital was definitely on the verge of open revolt against the Chinese.

Later that day, the Kshag implored the Dalai Lama to flee Lhasa. Urged on by his family — who had long ago decided that there was nothing to be gained by staying within reach of the PLA — Tenzin Gyatso agreed.

In his last hours in the Norbulingka, the Dalai Lama attended to his final responsibilities. He wrote letters giving his support to the leaders of the rebellion and instructed the armed groups not to make a stand in Lhasa, but instead to retreat to the south and fight the Chinese there. Then, changing into the robe of an ordinary Tibetan, he sat down on his meditation cushion to read a sermon in which Buddha charges his disciples to be courageous. Finally he rose and took from the wall a favourite painting of a Buddhist goddess and protector. He placed it in a special sack, draped it on his back, and left his living quarters. Completing his disguise by removing his glasses and slinging a borrowed rifle across his shoulder, he proceeded to the Norbulingka's gates. There he was joined by members of his Kshag and other palace officials, and together they stepped outside, unrecognized.

A throng of Tibetans gathers below the Potala in March 1959, just prior to the outbreak of open rebellion in Lhasa. The Lhasa uprising was ignited when the Chinese authorities asked the Dalai Lama to go unaccompanied to a PLA military base. Lhasans, fearing a kidnap attempt, attacked Chinese troops, who responded by shelling civilians.

A heavy dust storm was kicking up from the high plateau near Lhasa, providing the Dalai Lama and his party the cover they needed as they mounted their horses and rode out of the city. They headed south, towards the Tsangpo river and, just across it, the small monastery of Rame. There they made their first stop to await the Dalai Lama's family.

Once his family arrived and was ready to continue the journey, the party rode out of Rame, still heading south. Now their goal was India. Most in the group were old travelling companions, having been part of Tenzin Gyatso's entourage during the rather more official expedition to Beijing. The Dalai Lama's two tutors, Ling Rinpoche and Trijiang Rinpoche, were there, as were his mother, older sister, and P. T. Takala with his troops from the royal guard. The Dalai Lama's 14-year-old brother, Ngari Rinpoche, thought he was having the adventure of a lifetime as he rode along, weighed down by a Luger pistol and 200 bullets in the belligerent hope of shooting it out with a Chinese patrol. Tenzin Gyatso himself was supremely euphoric, overjoyed at last to be beyond the reach of the Chinese and able to speak his mind.

Pausing only at night, the travelers were met by bands of Khampa guerrillas who came to receive the Dalai Lama's blessing before returning to fight the Chinese. Also at night, there were meetings between the Dalai Lama and his advisers to discuss their future strategy. It was decided that they would establish a base at Lhuntse Dzong, a large fort on a hilltop 60 miles from the Indian border. Settling down with his party in the fort, the Dalai Lama planned to negotiate a settlement with the Chinese that would avoid any major bloodshed.

On March 19, two days after his departure from Lhasa, the Chinese realized that the Dalai Lama had fled. They dissolved the Tibetan government, sent detachments of the PLA in pursuit of the Dalai Lama, and ordered the southern border sealed to keep him from escaping into Bhutan or India. Tenzin Gyatso learned of these developments from intercepted radio messages. There was no time to lose:

He and his party would have to make a run for the border before the Chinese sealed it off completely.

The initial euphoria of escape was replaced by the frantic anxiety of flight. The Dalai Lama and his party made their way over some of the highest mountain passes in the world, a difficult feat made even harder by the dysentery from which he and many of his companions were suffering. At one point a Chinese plane flew over them, and fearing that they had been located the travellers broke up into separate groups. They regrouped in the last settlement in Tibet, the village of Mangmang, where they paused while scouts went ahead to check for Chinese patrols at the border.

In Mangmang the travellers found several other refugees from Lhasa who told of the PLA's actions in the days that followed the discovery of the Dalai Lama's flight. On the night of March 19, the Chinese shelled the Norbulingka grounds, killing and wounding hundreds of people, and took possession of the grounds the next morning. Meanwhile in the city itself, brutal street fighting had broken out.

Disguised as a commoner, the fleeing Tenzin Gyatso (on the white horse) and his caravan head south toward the Indian border. The Dalai Lama slipped out of Lhasa on March 17, two days before the PLA learned of his flight and set out in pursuit. The Chinese were within a few miles of catching him when he reached India on March 31.

The Dalai Lama is welcomed
to India, his new home in exile, by an Indian official in
April 1959. Meanwhile, back
in Tibet, the PLA was crush-
ing the rebellion, killing an
estimated 87,000 Tibetans
in the process.

Units of the Tibetan army joined thousands of
poorly armed Tibetan civilians and monks, who
tried to storm buildings held by Chinese troops. The
PLA cut down the attackers by the hundreds. On
the morning of March 21, the Tibetans achieved
their only success when a band of Khampas suc-
ceeded in overcoming the 100 Chinese troops sheltered in Lhasa's only cinema hall.

The last stand of the Lhasa revolt took place in
Tsuglakhang Temple, where the Dalai Lama had
rehearsed his debate with his examiners only a week
before. By the third day of fighting the temple and
its grounds were filled with more than 10,000 men,
women, and children seeking shelter from the car-
nage outside. Early on the morning of March 22,
the Chinese began shelling the temple, and by noon
the PLA was finally able to overrun the last defend-
ers. By that time hundreds more Tibetan and
Chinese dead littered the streets of Lhasa. The fighting continued another two days, but by then all

resistance had been crushed. As Chinese soldiers massacred Tibetan civilians in the capital, Chinese artillery bombarded Sera and Drepung, killing scores of monks trapped in the centuries-old monasteries.

As the Dalai Lama lay on his sickbed in Mangmang and heard the news of the bloodshed he had tried to avert for so long, he learned of more bad news: Chinese troops had already entered the nearby village of Tsona. He roused himself as his party prepared for an immediate departure. They would make the final dash for the Indian border.

On the afternoon of March 31, 1959, Tenzin Gyatso, mounted on a black yak, arrived at an Indian border post with 80 of his followers. He was received by a contingent of Indian troops who presented him with a silk scarf, a ceremonial Buddhist greeting. They then opened the gate and ushered him into India.

The Dalai Lama had become an exile.

7

The Exile of the God-King

As he descended through the Indian foothills, Tenzin Gyatso began to emerge from the daze of sickness, unhappiness, and anxiety that had engulfed him during his flight from Tibet. It was still a week's march before they could reach the first road or railway, but on the way the Dalai Lama was met by a government official carrying a welcoming telegram from the Indian prime minister, Jawaharlal Nehru.

When the Dalai Lama and his companions finally arrived at the town of Tezpur they were stunned to find almost a hundred reporters awaiting them, along with thousands of telegrams from well-wishers. The Dalai Lama gave the journalists a carefully worded statement — later known as the Tezpur statement — presenting a simple account of the tragic events in his country and expressing his regret over the bloodshed in Lhasa.

Nobody could have remained quite despondent after the sympathy I received as soon as we reached the first villages and towns in India.
—TENZIN GYATSO
THE DALAI LAMA
on reaching India in 1959

The Dalai Lama in exile in India. No longer able to play a direct role in events in Tibet, Tenzin Gyatso concentrated on bringing his homeland's plight to the attention of the world and on ministering to the needs of the thousands of Tibetan refugees who poured into India and Nepal.

The 23-year-old Dalai Lama
and his advisers in Tezpur,
India, in April 1959, 2 weeks
after his escape from PLA
forces in Tibet.

Two days later, the Beijing government issued a statement denouncing the Tezpur statement as a forgery "reflecting the will of the imperialist aggressors rather than the Dalai Lama himself." The term *imperialist aggressors* seemed to refer to the United States or perhaps Britain, both nations that at the time were antagonistic to China, although neither had had anything to do with the Tibetan rebellion. As the Chinese government continued to make allegations that the Dalai Lama had been kidnapped and was being held in India against his will, it became clear to Tenzin Gyatso that Mao Zedong, Zhou Enlai, and the rest of the Chinese leaders in Beijing approved of the PLA's actions in Tibet. Furthermore, the Panchen Lama had taken the Dalai Lama's place as the nominal leader of Tibet, moved into the Potala, and issued a statement condemning the rebels and giving his support to China's plans for transforming Tibet.

Soon after arriving in Tezpur, the Dalai Lama and his followers boarded a special train sent by the Indian government to transport them to Mussoorie, a town in the Himalayan foothills, just north of the Indian capital of New Delhi. They were received in Mussoorie by Prime Minister Nehru, who expressed his sympathy for the suffering of the Dalai Lama and his fellow Tibetans. But the Indian prime minister also told the Dalai Lama that the Tibetans could not expect any political or diplomatic support from India. The Indian government wanted to avoid provoking their Chinese neighbours, and when the Dalai Lama revealed his plans to maintain a government in exile, Nehru made it clear that India would not recognize it.

As the days passed in Mussoorie, the Dalai Lama became increasingly outspoken in his criticism of what the Chinese had done and were doing in his homeland. Refugees were now pouring out of Tibet by the thousands, forcing Tenzin Gyatso to see that, as he later put it, "the Chinese had made up their minds to subdue Tibet by sheer brutality." At a press conference in Mussoorie, the Dalai Lama formally repudiated the agreement that had bound his government to the Chinese since 1951. He also suggested that if the Chinese would allow an international commission to investigate the situation in Tibet he would gladly accept its verdict. Not surprisingly, the Chinese never responded to the suggestion.

His overtures to the Chinese government having proved futile, the Dalai Lama took the Tibetan case to the United Nations (UN) and the International Commission of Jurists, an organization made up of judges and lawyers from around the world. By now the scale of human suffering in Tibet was such that he was prepared to set aside the issue of his nation's independence and to limit his appeal to the upholding of the human rights of the Tibetan people.

Reports coming in from Tibetan refugees told of large-scale massacres and systematic executions that sometimes involved crucifixion, burning, strangulation, and live burial. Some independent sources estimated that as many as 87,000 Tibetans

I could not catch any glimpse of spiritual fervour in him, but I saw him as a brilliant practical statesman, with a masterly grasp of international politics, and he showed me that he had a profound love for his country and faith in his people.
—TENZIN GYATSO
THE DALAI LAMA
on Prime Minister
Jawaharlal Nehru of India

The Dalai Lama gives a press conference in India soon after his escape from Tibet. Beijing responded to his condemnation of the Chinese government's actions in Tibet by claiming that he had been kidnapped by the Western powers and was making accusations against China under duress.

had been killed in the uprising and the Chinese reprisals that ensued. Tibetan lamas in particular had been singled out by the Chinese authorities, whose communist government espoused a strict policy of atheism. Arguing that the monks had been "parasites" — a contention based on the monasteries' vast landholdings and powers of taxation — the Chinese now forced thousands of them to abandon their way of life, punishing, often with death, those who refused. To defuse Tibetan nationalism, the Chinese separated children from their parents and sent them to other Chinese provinces to be raised and educated. This programme of "detibetanization" involved thousands of children, from infants to teenagers.

After a number of meetings with various diplomats, the Dalai Lama finally prevailed upon two member nations of the UN, Ireland and Malaysia, to raise the issue of human rights abuses in Tibet in the UN General Assembly. The assembly eventually issued a mildly worded resolution calling for "respect for the fundamental human rights of the Tibetan people and for their distinctive cultural and religious life." Forty-five nations voted for the resolution, 9 against, and 26 abstained. The relative difficulty with which the mild resolution passed was the product of the rivalry between the communist and noncommunist nations; the Soviet Union and its allies felt bound to side with China, while the capitalist nations of the West, led by the United States, sought to use Tibet's tragedy as anticommunist propaganda. The resulting compromise had little, if any, impact on the Chinese, who were in any case not members of the UN at the time.

Shortly after the passing of the UN resolution, China faced much stronger criticism from a report by the International Commision of Jurists. The commision's report verified and catalogued the violence and bloodshed committed by the PLA against Tibetan civilians and confirmed that tens of thousands had been killed. The report also condemned the destruction being done to Tibetan culture under Chinese occupation. Hundreds of monasteries, which were virtually storehouses of Tibet's art and literature as well as of its religious traditions, had been destroyed by the PLA. Accordingly, the commission's report stated that the Chinese were guilty of "the gravest crime of which any person or nation can be accused — the intent to destroy a national, racial, or religious group as such."

Despite the stinging verdict of the jurists, the Tibetan cause received little effective support from the United States, Britain, or any other of the world's noncommunist powers — largely because no nation had much to gain by supporting the Dalai Lama's government. The Chinese were so strongly entrenched in Tibet's rugged terrain that it would have required a considerable military effort to dislodge them. Moreover, the greatest external threat posed by the Chinese presence in Lhasa was to India, a neutral country that had tried to steer clear of the U.S.-USSR rivalry. And the Indian government itself still hoped to establish cordial relations with the Chinese — a hope that soon would soon be dashed when China used its military outposts in the Himalayas to stage attacks against India during a brief border war in 1962.

I was not afraid of being one of the victims of the Chinese attack. But I knew my people and the officials of my government could not share my feelings. To them the person of the Dalai Lama was supremely precious. . . . They were convinced that if my body perished at the hands of the Chinese, the life of Tibet would also come to end.
—TENZIN GYATSO
THE DALAI LAMA
March 1959

The Dalai Lama meets with Indian prime minister Nehru in 1960. India generously provided for the Tibetan refugees and granted asylum to Tenzin Gyatso, but it accepted China's claim on Tibet in order to maintain good relations with Beijing. Behind Nehru is his daughter Indira Gandhi, who would later serve as prime minister (1966–77 and 1980–84).

No longer able to alter the course of events in Tibet, the Dalai Lama now faced a new and difficult responsibility. Nearly 100,000 refugees had already fled Tibet, almost all of them by the difficult overland route taken by Tenzin Gyatso. However, most of the refugees had not had the provisions enjoyed by the Dalai Lama; many were in poor health when they reached India, which had few facilities to treat the arriving refugees. Unaccustomed to the heat of the Indian plains and exhausted from the strain of the long trek from their native villages, the refugees fell prey to sickness and disease in their first days in India. They died by the hundreds.

Whatever the Indian government may have denied the Tibetans in terms of political support against China, they seemed willing to make up for in assisting the refugees. India set up two large refugee camps to gather and care for the incoming Tibetans. The Indian government found temporary work for many of the refugees in road construction all over northern India. Finally, the New Delhi government approached the Dalai Lama to offer a site for a new home for the Tibetans in exile.

The site of the new Tibetan "capital" in India was the town of Dharamsala, high in the pine-covered Dhauladhar range of the western Himalayas. Dharamsala was a largely abandoned "hill station," or resort, used by the British during their rule of India, which had ended in 1948. At first, the Dalai Lama was distressed at the distance of the site from New Delhi. But Dharamsala had many advantages. The altitude and climate were well suited to the Tibetans and, as the Dalai Lama soon realized, the refugee community would not be subjected to the constant poverty that other refugee populations had to endure. If the Tibetans had to live in exile, at least they would retain their dignity.

Lamas meet below the ruins of a monastery in Tibet, one of many dynamited by the Chinese during the 1960s. Monks and nuns formed the backbone of the resistance to the Chinese occupation authorities, who had confiscated the vast landholdings of the monasteries in the 1950s.

On April 29, 1960, after living for nearly a year in Mussoorie, Tenzin Gyatso took up residence in Dharamsala. Settling with his family and closest advisers into an old British bungalow, he spent his first days exploring the mountain trails around his new home.

Life in Dharamsala offered the Dalai Lama greater opportunity to pursue his religious tasks than he had known in years. Perhaps more important, it gave the Tibetan refugee community the chance to re-create the Tibetan culture and way of life; if the exiles could maintain a miniature Tibetan society they would prevent the Chinese from legitimizing their rule in Tibet itself. In a "little Tibet" in exile, the Dalai Lama hoped, Tibetans would prove that they could successfully modernize and reform their society, if they were only freed from Chinese domination.

To start with, an effective governing body had to be created. Accordingly, a new Kshag was established, with six ministries: home affairs, foreign affairs, religion and culture, education, finance, and security. A liaison office was established in New Delhi to maintain contact with the Indian government, and foreign offices were set up in Geneva, Switzerland; Kathmandu, Nepal; New York; and Tokyo to ensure that the world did not forget the Tibetan cause. Finally, the Dalai Lama decided that a new and democratic constitution should be drawn up, which would also serve as the model for the future constitution of a free Tibet.

Working together with a team of Indian constitutional lawyers (India was and remains the world's most populous democracy), the Dalai Lama and his Tibetan advisers went to work. They emerged with a constitution that blended communist principles of equal ownership and distribution of wealth with the procedures of representative democracy. No longer would high government positions be solely the property of the aristocratic families or incarnate lamas, at least in principle.

While the reforms were generally welcomed by the refugee community, Tenzin Gyatso's democratic zeal was occasionally a little too radical for Tibetan

tastes. For example, one article of the new constitution provided for the impeachment of the Dalai Lama by a two-thirds majority of the exiled Tsongdu. Opposition to this was so strong that 150 representatives of the new Tsongdu refused to accept the constitution unless the clause was removed. Ultimately, however, the Dalai Lama's powers of persuasion prevailed, and the impeachment article remained in the document. "If we were to have a true democracy," he later said, "there had to be provisions whereby the Dalai Lama's powers could also be changed."

The first election in the refugee community was held only months after the Dalai Lama had settled in at Dharamsala, and it was an unusual one indeed. Most of the refugees had never had any opportunity to participate in a political process before; stranger yet, no candidates formally ran for office.

A Tibetan mother and child, who had fled Tibet for northeastern India in 1959, in an Indian refugee camp in 1962; they were displaced from their home in exile by a brief border war between India and China. By the end of the 1960s, more than 100,000 Tibetan refugees were living in India.

An exiled Tibetan monk in Dharamsala, India, repairs a page from an ancient Tibetan religious book. Many of the monks who fled their homeland brought such texts with them to Dharamsala, which became the centre of the Tibetan exile community.

Instead, people were simply asked to write down the name of a fellow exile from their own region of Tibet whom they respected as a leader. Thirteen representatives were chosen from the lists, which were collected from Tibetan camps all over India, and these 13 men composed the first popularly elected Tibetan parliament. This first group of representatives were all either aristocrats, high lamas, or tribal chieftans. More formal elections were held in 1963 and then regularly at three-year intervals.

Tenzin Gyatso was now a bona fide political reformer, as well as a highly respected author in the Western world; his book, *My Land and My People*, published in 1962, was well received in North America and Great Britain and was instrumental in publicizing the plight of Tibet. But he still retained his traditional role in Tibetan society, and Tibetan refugees often wept when they saw him dressed in the robes of an ordinary lama; for the Tibetans who had been raised to revere the Dalai Lama as the incarnation of Chenrezi, it was deeply upsetting to see him behaving like an ordinary political leader.

In time, as conditions in the refugee community improved, Tenzin Gyatso was able to return to a life that was more in tune with his people's expectations of a Dalai Lama. In 1968, a new residence was established for him: the Thekchen Choling, or "Island of the Mahayana Teaching." Like the Norbulingka in Lhasa it was really a large park that contained a modest private cottage for the Dalai Lama within its walls. Around the Thekchen Choling runs the Lingkhor, a re-creation of the Holy Walk of the same name in Lhasa, along which devout Tibetans would circulate every day as a religious penance. The Dalai Lama's personal monastery, Namgyal Dratsang, was also re-created in Dharamsala, along with a new central temple where Tenzin Gyatso occasionally held services.

He also established a rigorous daily routine for himself, which he adhered to for the next 20 years. Upon rising at 4:00 A.M., the Dalai Lama would spend half an hour in solitary contemplation in his garden, follow it with a light breakfast, then spend another hour seated in motionless meditation. Next he consulted the morning newspapers and radio and television reports on Tibet, including transcripts of transmissions from Radio Lhasa and Radio Beijing. He then retired to his study to immerse himself in Buddhist scriptures. (His instructors in scriptural studies since childhood, Trijiang Rinpoche and Ling Rinpoche, continued to serve as his tutors until their respective deaths in 1981 and 1984.) His afternoons were consumed by audiences with the numerous foreigners who came to Dharamsala to speak with him, and at least twice a week he held meetings with his top ministers.

But apart from this daily routine, Tenzin Gyatso also spent a great deal of time travelling to visit the many Tibetan exile communities in India. He also ventured abroad on several occasions, both to keep the Tibetan cause in the eye of the international public and to conduct ceremonies for Buddhists from Canada to Mongolia. In 1967, the Indian government allowed him to visit Japan, a country with many adherents to Buddhism, and in 1973 he made a six-week-long tour of Europe that included a meeting with Pope Paul VI, the religious leader of the world's Roman Catholics. In 1971, he asked the U.S. government to allow him to visit the United States but was turned down — at the time the Americans were seeking to open relations with China and did not want to jeopardize that delicate process by playing host to the exiled leader opposed to the Chinese occupation of his country. But by 1979, U.S.-Chinese relations were fully normalized, and the American government finally issued the Dalai Lama a visa to tour the United States as a private citizen. He arrived in New York and met with its tiny Tibetan community and the city's religious leaders. He visited a number of Buddhist temples around the country, spoke at 15 universities from Harvard to UCLA, and addressed several major U.S. foreign policy groups to subtly plead his nation's cause.

Throughout this period, a great deal was done in the Tibetan exile community to revive and safeguard Tibet's religious and cultural traditions. Several monasteries were set up at different sites in India, many of them replicas of the major lamaseries of

[Chinese leader] Deng Xiaoping has the courage to admit mistakes. In the past it was rare for the top Chinese leadership to speak with such realism about political matters. If China's leaders are now sincere about change, and hold to it for a generation, that will be very good, but I really doubt that they will.
—TENZIN GYATSO
THE DALAI LAMA

Tibet. The Dalai Lama also established a programme to preserve as much of Tibet's religious literature as possible, much of which the Chinese had begun to systematically destroy. Those manuscripts and books that were smuggled out of Tibet were now collected and painstakingly lithographed and copied. As a result, by 1984 more than 50,000 volumes, representing perhaps 40 percent of Tibet's religious literature, were stored in the newly built Library of Tibetan Works and Archives in Dharamsala.

Whatever success the Dalai Lama and the Tibetan community in general had in reestablishing their political and cultural institutions was more than matched by the refugees' success in establishing their economic independence. During the 1960s, a number of farming communities were set up by the Tibetans on land donated by the Indian government. By the end of the 1980s, they were thriving communities that provided a livelihood for thou-

Tenzin Gyatso opens a Tibet House cultural centre in the Indian capital of New Delhi in the 1980s. The Dalai Lama travelled throughout Europe, North America, and much of Asia in the 1970s and 1980s to protest human rights violations in his homeland and to promote the establishment of Tibetan cultural centres.

sands of Tibetans. Many others became traders, and in any city or major town in India or Nepal (the predominantly Hindu nation that was home to more than 14,000 Tibetan exiles in the late 1980s) one can be sure to find a prosperous Tibetan market selling anything from traditional Tibetan daggers to fashionable woollen sweaters.

The Tibetan refugees had staged a remarkable recovery over the two decades of their exile. During that period, the international reaction to the plight of Tibet had grown from apathy to wide public awareness. By 1989, a Tibetan cultural centre was under construction in New York, and American newspapers and television networks ran frequent reports on the situation in Tibet.

But in the province of Xizang, since 1965 the official Chinese name for Tibet, the occupation dragged on. And among the Tibetans who remained behind in their homeland, the hatred for the Chinese occupiers grew more and more intense with each passing year.

A Tibetan merchant works in his store in Nepal — like India a predominantly Hindu nation — in the early 1970s. After an initial period of poverty and dislocation, Tibetan exiles in India and Nepal prospered in small business. The exile community as a whole was dedicated to keeping alive traditional Tibetan Buddhist culture.

8

The Long Journey of Rebirth

As the Tibetan exiles established themselves and their culture in their new home in the early 1960s, the Dalai Lama's life and work inevitably revolved more around them than around the struggle for Tibet itself. There was little he could do except persevere in his attempts to gain international attention for the plight of the Tibetans.

Yet despite his belief that he was the reincarnation of the bodhisattva of supreme compassion, the Dalai Lama offered some measure of approval for those who took up arms against the Chinese. Indeed, he would quote old Buddhist fables to argue that violence was justifiable "if a person's motivation as well as the result of his actions are solely for the benefit of the majority of the people." All the same, this was clearly not his chosen path. More characteristic was his observation that "we should not seek revenge on those who have committed crimes against us, or reply to those crimes with

In Buddism, you should not mind those who make you angry. You should love those people who irritate you, because they are your gurus. In that sense the Chinese are our gurus.
—TENZIN GYATSO
THE DALAI LAMA
July 1969

The Dalai Lama in his home in Dharamsala in 1989, 30 years after he fled Tibet. Forced into a political role by events beyond his control, he nevertheless remained a deeply spiritual man during his many years in exile.

other crimes." Instead, he said, "We should reflect that by the law of Karma they are in danger of lowly and miserable lives to come, and our duty toward them, as to every being, is to help them rise toward Nirvana [enlightenment] rather than to let them sink to lower levels of rebirth."

In the early 1960s, groups of Khampas began a long, intermittent guerrilla war against isolated PLA garrisons from mountain bases along the Tibet-Nepal border. The rebel military activity was relatively minor, but it provided Beijing with a pretext for refusing to negotiate with the Dalai Lama's government in exile. Meanwhile, the Chinese government began to settle large numbers of ethnic Chinese farmers and workers in Tibet.

Young Chinese carry posters supporting Mao Zedong and exhorting their nation to return to the principles of orthodox communism during a march in Beijing in 1966, the first year of China's Cultural Revolution. The nationwide jailings, purges, and destruction of institutions that accompanied the Cultural Revolution wracked Tibet as well.

In the mid-1960s, Tibet was engulfed in what the Chinese called the Cultural Revolution, a long period of turmoil and violence that consumed all of China. Initiated by Mao to solidify his increasingly shaky base of power, the Cultural Revolution was on the surface an effort to reclaim the original principles of the Chinese Communist revolution that brought Mao to power. Bands of young Communists known as the Red Guards seized anyone they suspected of "incorrect thought" and forced them to make public confessions. Tens of thousands of people were jailed for their alleged "crimes against the revolution," from high party officials, leading writers and scientists, people who had managed to accumulate some wealth, and those who practised their religion, to ordinary citizens who just happened to have been in the wrong place at the wrong time. The Red Guards also swept through the cities and countryside, ransacking university buildings, temples and shrines, farms, and the homes of those they considered guilty.

Tibet was almost entirely cut off from the rest of the world during the Cultural Revolution, as the Red Guards purged the province of "impurity." Chinese political workers organized groups of young Tibetans from the poorest peasant classes into a political faction known as the Gyenlog, a Tibetan version of the Red Guards. The Gyenlog youths were encouraged to destroy what were referred to as the Four Olds: old thought, old culture, old habits, and old customs. Hundreds of Tibet's ancient monasteries and nunneries were laid waste in a few years, their scriptures burned, their statues and images melted down, and their walls sometimes dynamited. The Potala was used as a school, then made into a museum, the treasures it contained intended to illustrate to common Tibetans the greed of the old religious hierarchy.

Ironically, the Cultural Revolution also claimed as its victims many of the commanders and political officials who had first established Chinese power in Tibet. Thus, it must have been with some satisfaction that Tibetans heard the news of the downfall of Zhang Jingwu, the general who had met the Dalai

While the Chinese said the Cabinet was in league with the Khampa guerrillas, I have no doubt the Khampas believed the Cabinet was more or less in league with the Chinese.
—TENZIN GYATSO
THE DALAI LAMA
on the political situation
after the outbreak of the
Khampa rebellion

A group of Tibetan nomad women churn butter in the 1970s. The Chinese occupiers profoundly changed the face of Tibetan agriculture, forcing nomads to settle in fixed communities and peasants to grow crops for export to China instead of traditional Tibetan crops. Such policies resulted in food shortages in Tibet.

Lama in Yatung as Beijing's first representative to occupied Tibet. But such indirect revenge was small comfort in the face of the continuing chaos in Tibet itself. Quite apart from the hundreds of thousands of lamas who were displaced during the Cultural Revolution, the Gyenlog also began a systematic attack on religion in general, punishing any Tibetan who attempted to practise his or her faith. The Gyenlog also forced Tibetan peasants to pool their land for "collective agriculture," a system that had been efficient in densely populated China but was not as well suited to Tibet, which had an abundance of surplus farmland. The Tibetan farmers were coerced into abandoning their traditional crops to grow wheat instead — a staple food for the 400,000 Chinese who had settled in Tibet, but one that Tibetans had never grown or eaten. The Tibetans had great difficulty maintaining supplies of their own food crops, and by the late 1960s they were facing famine conditions.

As the situation worsened, the Chinese authorities faced dissent from Tibetan leaders within their own camp. The Panchen Lama in particular had begun to express his discontent with the suppression of religion in Tibet. Finally in 1964, the

Panchen Lama, now 27, made a speech to a vast crowd in Lhasa's main square, declaring that "Tibet will soon regain her independence" and that "his Holiness the Dalai Lama will return to the Golden Throne." The authorities were quick to respond, placing the Panchen Lama under house arrest, and shortly thereafter bringing him and his closest advisers to trial. After an elabourate judicial process — he was accused of crimes ranging from adultery to raising a guerrilla army — the Panchen Lama was pronounced guilty and imprisoned. He would not be released for another 14 years.

The Cultural Revolution lasted three years and came to an end in 1968. In its aftermath in the early 1970s, a new wave of rebellions spread across Tibet. The PLA, fearing an uprising like that of 1959, stepped in to suppress the Gyenlog and made some efforts to repair the damage done during the Cultural Revolution, but the Tibetan resistance continued to oppose the occupation. In 1974, when the Chinese government put pressure on Nepal to put a stop to the Khampas' activities, the Nepalese asked

A modern apartment house of Chinese design stands in stark contrast to the nearby Potala, which was turned into a museum in the 1960s. By the end of the 1980s, nearly 1 million ethnic Chinese were living in Tibet. Mandarin Chinese was the sole language used in Tibetan schools, part of an effort to eradicate Tibetan nationalism.

Tenzin Gyatso to appeal to the guerrillas for a cease-fire. The Dalai Lama, anxious to maintain good relations between the Tibetan exile community in Nepal and the Nepalese government, urged the guerrillas to surrender to the Nepalese; those who did were locked up in Nepalese jails for the better part of the next decade.

Both Mao and Zhou died in 1976, bringing more moderate leaders to power in Beijing. In February 1978, they approved the release of the Panchen Lama from prison, and shortly thereafter they invited the Dalai Lama to send a series of delegations to visit Tibet. In September 1979, the first of these delegations, which included the Dalai Lama's brother Lobsang Samten, departed for Lhasa. The delegates were instructed by their Chinese hosts to avoid contact with the public for security reasons, but they found it impossible to comply. As Tenzin Gyatso's representatives arrived in the capital, they were mobbed by 17,000 Tibetans. Despite warnings from the police, hundreds followed them whenever they appeared in the streets. When the delegates were taken to visit the Norbulingka, now renamed People's Park, they were once again greeted by a crowd of thousands chanting slogans in praise of the Dalai Lama. Similar scenes occurred wherever the delegation travelled in Tibet.

It had been 20 years since anyone in those crowds had been a subject of the Dalai Lama's, and many were too young to remember the time when he ruled. Yet the presence of his representatives inspired the largest public acts of defiance Tibet had seen in years. They would be surrounded by weeping crowds who begged for their blessings as the Dalai Lama's representatives, and the delegates themselves were often overcome with emotion at the reception they received from their countrymen. At times these scenes even moved their Chinese guides to tears.

Two more delegations, which included Tenzin Gyatso's other brothers and sisters, followed in the early 1980s and received equally tumultuous welcomes. But the delegates were getting increasingly upset at the poverty and the results of the destruc-

In spite of the atrocious crimes which the Chinese have committed in our country, I have absolutely no hatred in my heart of the Chinese people. I believe it is one of the curses and dangers of the present age to blame nations for the crimes of individuals.

—TENZIN GYATSO
THE DALAI LAMA

tion they saw in their homeland. Meanwhile, the local crowds that greeted them were becoming increasingly militant, often shouting slogans demanding Tibetan independence from China. Consequently, the Chinese authorities cut short the visit of the third delegation and called off the scheduled visit of a fourth delegation indefinitely. The last significant contact between the Chinese government and the Dalai Lama's government in exile occurred in 1982, when several members of the Dharamsala Kshag flew to Beijing to discuss the status of Tibet with high-level Chinese officials. The talks made no progress, and there was no contact between Beijing and the Tibetan exile government through the rest of the 1980s.

An Indian policeman tries to restrain a Tibetan protester during a demonstration outside the Chinese embassy in New Delhi in 1987. The pro-independence guerrilla movement inside Tibet grew in strength throughout the 1980s.

However, the Chinese government did take advantage of Westerners' long fascination with Tibet by opening it to foreign tourists. In the early part of the decade, tourists could reach Tibet only via China, but in 1986 the Chinese authorities allowed tourists to enter through Nepal. One American woman told of sneaking a dozen postcards of the Dalai Lama across the border — his photo is banned by the Chinese authorities — and trading them with Tibetans for turquoise-embellished belts and other intricately handcrafted items. When shown the Dalai Lama's picture, she reported, several Tibetans were overcome with emotion; some even fell to their knees.

The Chinese occupation of Tibet remained rigid and unyielding throughout the 1980s despite the many reforms, including a small amount of free speech, instituted throughout the People's Republic of China in the early part of the decade by its leader Deng Xiaoping. More than 500,000 Chinese civilians had been settled in central Tibet and provided with living conditions far superior to those available to the Tibetan population. Tibetan culture was still under systematic attack, and even the Tibetan language was suppressed; as late as 1989, all secondary education in Tibet was taught in Mandarin Chinese.

Tibetans loot a Chinese restaurant during rioting in Lhasa in March 1989, the fourth time major disturbances had broken out in the capital in 18 months. Scores were killed during the 1989 rioting, which prompted the Chinese authorities to declare martial law in the Lhasa region for the first time in 30 years.

In 1983, a number of public executions of counter-revolutionaries, a term the Chinese used for Tibetan nationalists, were carried out in Lhasa. More nationalists were executed in September 1987, prompting a short but violent revolt in Lhasa, where hundreds of lamas rioted and burned down a police station. Chinese police and soldiers ultimately quelled the revolt, but according to unofficial reports dozens of people were killed, mostly Tibetans. The Chinese government blamed the unrest on "intrigues by the Dalai Lama clique."

In the year and a half that followed, Lhasa was the scene of several major demonstrations demanding more religious freedom and an end to Chinese oppression. In March 1988, a massive demonstration involving some 10,000 Lhasans developed into a riot and resulted in the death of at least 18 monks and an unknown number of other Tibetans and Chinese policemen. The violence began on the morning of the final day of the Monlam festival. According to reports pieced together from eyewitness accounts, a group of about 200 monks at the Jokhang Cathedral started to chant pro-independence slogans and throw stones at Chinese police. Soon thousands of civilians joined in and ran to a police station, sacking it, beating policemen, and, according to one report, throwing two policemen from the top floor of the building. The police apparently responded by firing into the crowd. According to eyewitnesses, most of the monks were killed when they were hurled by police from the top of the Jokhang, which the monks had stormed and held briefly.

There was more violence in December 1988: 18 Tibetans were killed and 130 wounded when Chinese police opened fire on marchers denouncing human-rights violations in Tibet. According to eyewitness reports, the marchers were led by a group of monks and nuns carrying the outlawed Tibetan flag. March 1989 saw the fourth pro-independence demonstration in Lhasa to end in bloodshed in 18 months, and it was the most serious episode yet. Anti-Chinese rioting continued for 3 days, with some unofficial reports putting the death toll at as many as 100 people, most of them Tibetans. The

My people are suffering terribly for want of basic things like food, shelter, and the freedom to move about. . . . The problem is not religion, ideology, or racism by the Chinese, but the fact that they treat us as inferiors. . . . I will not return until the people say they are satisfied with their society.
—TENZIN GYATSO
THE DALAI LAMA
on the terms of his return
to Tibet

A group of Tibetan refugees living in the Indian protectorate of Sikkim hold rosaries and prayer wheels. Tibetans both inside and outside Tibet persisted in the devout practice of Buddhism, and they continued to revere the Dalai Lama as a reincarnation of the divine bodhisattva of supreme compassion.

Chinese government declared a state of martial law in Lhasa and its environs — the first time since 1959 that martial law had been declared in Tibet. Several regiments of the PLA moved into the capital, all foreign tourists were ordered out of the city, and house-to-house searches resulted in mass arrests of Tibetans suspected of pro-independence activities.

The events of the late 1980s caused public opinion in the United States, Canada, Britain, and elsewhere in the West to run decidedly against the Chinese occupation, but Western governments, hoping to cultivate friendly relations and business contacts with China, said nothing about Beijing's treatment of Tibet. The Chinese pro-government newspaper *China Daily*, meanwhile, explained the 1989 imposition of martial law in Tibet by saying that the rioting in Lhasa "is certainly not a sign of anything but blind hatred on the part of the [Tibetan] separatists — a far cry from the responsibility

required if there is to be a rational dialogue and
practical solution to whatever problems exist in Tibet." The Chinese government did at least admit
that in the past it had been perhaps a bit too heavy-
handed in Tibet, but blamed the excesses on
Maoists who remained in the Chinese government.
Similar sentiments were voiced by the Panchen
Lama, who reemerged as a defender of the Chinese
occupiers before his death from heart failure in January 1989.

Outside Tibet, the Tibetan exile community has
continued to actively express outrage at the treatment inflicted upon their homeland. They have
staged protests the world over, from UN headquar-
ters in New York to the Chinese embassy gates in
New Delhi. During the 1970s, many young exiles
thought the time had come for a renewed struggle
through a terrorist campaign against the People's
Republic of China. They had got as far as setting

up training camps for guerrilla fighters, but the effort lost momentum with the first signs of liberalization in China in the early 1980s. Nevertheless, a military reserve force still existed in the form of an all-Tibetan commando unit in the Indian army, patrolling the mountainous border between Tibet and India.

As the 1980s drew to a close, Tenzin Gyatso continued to live in the hope that he would one day return to Lhasa. He had no illusions that the Tibet to which he might one day return could ever be the same as the land he once knew. And despite the hopes of many young Tibetans, he saw little prospect for an independent Tibet in the near future. But he did continue to hope that China would make good its long-standing promise to grant Tibet true regional autonomy and the right to conduct its own internal affairs. In June 1988, for example, he publicly proposed that China grant Tibet internal autonomy and even retain the right to station some troops in the province. By making the proposal, the Dalai Lama was implicitly accepting China's claim on Tibet, the first time he had ever done so. But Beijing rejected his proposal, claiming that it was "aimed at undermining China's territorial integrity."

Lhasans surround the body of a lama killed by Chinese police during the March 1989 rioting. The marking of traditional religious festivals, when monks and nuns from all over Tibet converge on Lhasa, often sparked anti-Chinese, pro-independence unrest. Though world public opinion backed the Tibetans, most nations refused to condemn China.

The Dalai Lama's moderate stance has earned him some criticism from a number of Tibetan nationalists, but he has continued his search for, as he called it, a "middle way" in Tibet. In a 1988 interview he described that search: "Not complete independence, but equal status and mutual respect, and our own land within a republic of China where we are master and China is helper. . . . I am not much concerned about terms like autonomy, independence, or republic."

He has been thrust into the role of a politician, but first and foremost Tenzin Gyatso is the Dalai Lama — the spiritual leader of millions of Buddhists and one of the world's leading theologians. He remains a deeply religious man whose primary concern is the place of all living beings in both the material and the spiritual realm. In 1988, *Life* magazine asked him to summarize for American readers his religion's view of the meaning of life. "According to Buddhism," he answered,

> there are a limitless number of universes. . . . In this vastness, can we ever know why we are here? From the Buddhist point of view, our consciousness has the potential to know every object. Because of obstructions we are, at present, unable to know everything. However, by removing the obstructions gradually, it is ultimately possible to know everything.
>
> . . . All living beings strive to sustain their lives so that they might achieve happiness. As to why the self, wishing for happiness, came into being, Buddhism answers: This self has existed from beginningless time. It has no end but for it to ultimately achieve full enlightenment.

Some Tibetans believe an ancient prophecy that says the 14th Dalai Lama will be the last of the incarnations of Chenrezi. But the same prediction states that the Tibetan people will regain their land, and for Tenzin Gyatso, that is the more important part of the prophecy.

Still, he has no doubt about his own reincarnation. "As long as there is suffering in the world," he once said, "I will be back."

Tenzin Gyatso has slowly come to accept China's rule over Tibet, but he has never abandoned his call for China to respect the human rights of Tibetans. He has vowed never to return to his homeland until limited self-rule has been restored. As the 1980s drew to a close, the Dalai Lama was respected throughout the world as a man of peace, eloquence, and deep spirituality.

Further Reading

Avedon, John F *In Exile from the Land of Snows: The First Full Account of the Dalai Lama and the Tibetans since the Chinese Conquest* Wisdom 1985

Bell, Charles *Portrait of a Dalai Lama: The Life and Times of the Great Thirteenth* Wisdom 1988

Harrer, Heinrich *Return to Tibet* Translated by Ewald Osers Penguin 1985

Hicks, Roger, and Ngakpa Chogyam *Great Ocean: An Authorized Biography of the Buddhist Monk Tenzin Gyatso* Element Books 1984

Kewley, Vanya *Tibet: Behind the Ice Curtain* Grafton 1990

Levinson, Claude B *Dalai Lama* Unwin Hyman 1988

Norbu, Thubten Jigme & Turnbull, Colin Macmillan *Tibet: Its History, Religion & People* Penguin 1976

Normanton, Simon *Tibet: The Lost Civilization* Hamish Hamilton 1988

Richardson, Hugh E *Tibet and Its History* Shambhala 1985

Tenzin Gyatso *Buddhism of Tibet* Allen & Unwin 1983

Tenzin Gyatso *Freedom in Exile: The Autobiography of the Dalai Lama* John Curtis/Hodder 1990

Wilby, Sorrel *Tibet: A Woman's Lone Trek Across a Mysterious Land* Macdonald 1988

Chronology

Aug. 1933	Thubten Gyatso, the 13th Dalai Lama, dies
July 1935	Lhamo Dhondrub, the future Tenzin Gyatso, born in Taktser, Tsinghai province, China
Winter 1937	Lhamo Dhondrub identified as the Dalai Lama by a Tibetan search party
Feb. 22, 1940	Lhamo Dhondrub, renamed Tenzin Gyatso, is officially installed in the Potala, the royal palace of the Dalai Lama, in Lhasa, Tibet
Aug. 1948	Participates in the debates at Drepung and Sera
Oct. 1950	Chinese forces invade Tibet
Nov. 17, 1950	Tenzin Gyatso made head of government
Dec. 1950	Flees Lhasa for Yatung; Chinese troops enter Lhasa
May 1951	China takes over Tibetan government
Aug. 1951	Tenzin Gyatso returns to Lhasa
Summer 1954	Visits China and meets with Chinese leader Mao Zedong
1955	Revolt in Kham begins
Nov. 1956	Tenzin Gyatso visits India to celebrate the 2,500th anniversary of the birth of the Buddha
June 1958	Kham revolt spreads to central Tibet
March 1959	Uprising against the Chinese in Lhasa begins; Tenzin Gyatso flees to India, and thousands of refugees follow; Panchen Lama named head of new Chinese regime in Lhasa; an estimated 87,000 Tibetans killed by Chinese troops
April 1960	Dalai Lama establishes Tibetan exile headquarters in Dharamsala, India; Chinese colonists start to settle in Tibet
1964	Chinese depose Panchen Lama as ruler of Tibet
1965	Tibet renamed Xizang province, directly governed by ethnic Chinese
1967	Destruction of Tibetan holy places intensifies during Chinese Cultural Revolution
1979	Tenzin Gyatso visits United States; first delegation from the Dalai Lama visits Lhasa
Aug. 1987	Pro-independence riots in Lhasa begin
June 1988	Dalai Lama proposes plan for limited autonomy of Tibet; recognizes China's claim to Tibet for the first time
March 1989	Tibetans riot in Lhasa for fourth time in 18 months; China declares martial law in Lhasa region

Index